THE BOOK OF BARKLEY

LOVE AND LIFE THROUGH THE EYES OF A LABRADOR RETRIEVER

Thank you for supporting
RainCoast Dog Rescue

L. B Johnson

L. B. JOHNSON

outskirtspress
DENVER, COLORADO

The Book of Barkley
Love and Life Through the Eyes of a Labrodor Retriever

v2.0 r1.1

Outskirts Press, Inc.
http://www.outskirtspress.com

ISBN: 978-1-4787-3434-5

PRINTED IN THE UNITED STATES OF AMERICA

To EJ – For Being There On The Best Parts Of The Journey

Table of Contents

1
The Book of Barkley

In rough wool socks, in a cooling room, I read from the books of the Old Testament, dipping my finger in a glass of whiskey, salvaging all I can from myth and truth, as reality comes through the window like a tossed brick.

Outside there was nothing, the world outside the window, only a long, steady dusting of snow, the dark and constant presence of winter's scorn. Somewhere in the distance, a snowplow scrapes the day's history from the streets as I pull a sweater around me, small comfort in this empty house.

We find comfort in various ways. For some, it's food, human warmth and need or the acquisition of possessions. For some, it's drugs or alcohol, a balm to the self we deceive ourselves into believing as being measurably containable. We're not though; days come in which we're like a glass too full, barely preventing ourselves from spilling over through surface tension.

Our comforts can be our healing, but if left unchecked, they can be our curse, carried in an empty bag, a broken bottle, harsh words that scatter like empty containers, the hiss of a snake as we toss it away. They can also be our savior, keeping us from that isolating inward spiral, the soul's needle that rips free the bindings, thus letting our wounds heal.

For me, my comfort this night is the written Word of God, of man, or a mere mortal woman, the thoughts in a journal that spring from my own day. Those words laid out unfolded, are my way of savoring what it means to be alive; and the most striking measure of life is the literal odds against it. For every way that there is of being here, humanity and nature have derived an infinite number of ways of not being here. Calamities of man and nature can wipe out entire civilizations even as the smallest of things can render us completely and totally undone, a meteorite and a microbe carrying the same weight. Statistics belittles our very existence; thermodynamics prohibits us, and gravity usually wins. That's *if* we're not taken out first by hurricane, flood, donkey accident, tainted food, terrorists or that offer of a ride home by that nice guy at the bar with an eye patch and a hook for a hand.

I spent much of my early adulthood as a jet pilot, learning very quickly that, not only can't you always save the world, sometimes you cannot even save yourself. But the effort is often worth it. If you're lucky, your brushes with life will only leave a few small physical scars. If I raise up my bangs, right at the hairline, there's a tiny, faint scar from a tumble off my bike down a hill as a kid. There's a small ding in my forehead where the bungee cord of the J60-P-3 turbojet engine cover whacked me on the ramp at warp speed when I lost the wrestling contest with it. But for most people, like me, the bigger scars are internal, and you only touch them softly, with trepidation, not remorse, in the late night hours of "what if's."

Pilots get that. Adventurers get that. So, usually, does anyone who has challenged their fears. There are times when it seems as if the world is going to pieces around you, a sense of this enormous elemental power beyond your reason or control. You think, "What am I doing; this is nuts!" As you squeak past the reaper one more time, you say "*well, that wasn't as bad as I thought*" already planning on when you will chase the experience again. For you are called to the altar of the infinite, the bread of life on the tongue, tasting faintly of salt, the sweetness, just underneath. It's reaching our hand out to receive glory even as your world cranks up to red line—with the knowledge that if mistakes are made, there will be no saving grace; you may be lost. But if you are not, then the world will, for that instant, have one moment of equilibrium, of order, of peace.

Those moments, perfect moments of transcendence, almost worthy of the reckoning.

It's moments like this, like these here now, that are our way of saying that, in the face of the impossible, life is worth savoring. It's acknowledging that when life lobs something our way like a grenade, shards of pain exploding across our world, that life still can be a gift, still a story to be told.

It is a story, not one of science, one that may not be remembered past this one lifetime. It is the story of someone that did not know his destiny, but followed it with unfaltering step, bound to me, not by vows or paper, but in the name of the trust that was the best part of his nature. It is a story of the one that taught me to love even as he occasionally barfed on my carpet. It is simply the tale of a black Labrador retriever named Barkley.

It was the beginning I never anticipated--belief that there were no limits that made tragedy inevitable, a gentle nuzzle that made the walls fall away, and the pull of the leash into the day's infinitude.

It was an ending I did not expect; a leash laid across the chair, an empty bed, a glass tipped over, spilling the blood of wine. The noise that empty rooms make is as clear as tears.

In between, there are the stories of friends, of joy and dog hair, of a small pink ball with feet known as Mr. Squeaky, which became my mortal enemy at dawn, as I tried to sleep. There are tales of the great "bacon incident" and how I know more about how to clean carpet than should be allowed by law. There are words that twist and turn in the shade of an ancient tree, a sonnet to an old dog, who lies between the bones of poets, to be unearthed as he releases me to remember.

A couch sits across from me, absent of a form that claimed it for ten years. Under the table, are a few favorite toys, sticks and stones that now break my bones, even as I cannot bear to part with them. I sit, the solitary dreamer, pulled to the perimeters of memory that can't yet be mapped. I sit, a cowboy without his sidekick, my defense laid down on the bar, nursing the hurt with one part tears and two parts single malt. Barkley's things are stacked by the door, as ordered as rifle cartridges, a dog's length from the barrel of the bottle. That bottle is a place I do not want to lose myself, I think as small sounds come from my chest, as the rumble of thunder infinitely remote, the vibration of grief down deep inside, tremulous and impartial and waiting.

But grieving with memories is better than nothing without them and the only thing worse than not being alive, is not having anything to remember.

So for tonight, I will simply pour a finger of warmth and put the bottle aside to sit, to wait for something I cannot name, but of which I can still remember. I will remember the alone as a white shirt on the line, fluttering in the hot wind. I'll remember the together as the sound of a puppy's whimper. I will remember it all as an open field under cloudless skies, as we learned to walk together, of fresh grass and soft ice cream, wood smoke and black powder, of black fur and white knights and love unexpected. I'll remember it and write of it, as a renouncement of pain, as a leap into unknown air, a dog, a moment, so worthy of the price.

Our wounds we wear like temporary garments until they are forgotten, but our stories, we don them as forever.

2

The Decision

It began with a dream of puppies, tumbling through clean grass, the tiny barks that spoke of new life, of fresh futures. I knew I had neither the time nor currently, a home fit for a puppy that would grow up into eighty or ninety pounds of fur and flesh, but I'd gone much of my adult life without one and I missed it. I knew it was impractical, and my family tried to talk me out of it. "You just have a little townhouse," "Who will take care of him when you travel?" and "You've got student loans from going back to graduate school and dogs are an expense!"

Still, it was my dream, and there was no talking me out of it.

As children we dream. Growing up where toys had actual moving parts outside of the video controller, our imaginations soared. We were cowboys; we were soldiers, spies, sailors, astronauts. We burst out of the house as flushed quail, rushing out of the grass with that unfaltering faith in our own liberty. We only came back when we were hungry or it got dark and Mom's call echoed to come inside.

On special nights, my big brother and I got to sleep outside in the pup tent, the yard behind the house, as large as it was, surrounded with a high fence, beyond which lay additional property that lapped up near the foothills of the mountains. He never minded his "little sis" tagging along on his adventures, and there was nothing we did not share. With us would be our dog, Pepper, a little wiener dog that was our constant companion and usually slept with one of us. As the flap of the tent breathed in and out, I could smell the trees outside and I smiled as I drifted off to sleep, thinking, as a child does, that I'd never be alone.

Inside that fence, with our courageous dog to guard us, we were safe from wandering deer, raccoons or the monsters that existed only in our imaginations. The back door was unlocked; a small light left on, in case I had to come in and use the bathroom, a jug of water and some plastic cups on the picnic table if we got thirsty. I remember pouring a cup, there in the dark, watching the water swirl around, only the reflections of two solitary stars on its dark surface.

We'd lie in that tent and talk, of what we were going to buy with the allowance we earned from doing extra chores, of what manner of goop had been served in the school cafeteria on Thursday ("sounded like Spamalope patties to me, Big Bro") and what we might want to be when we grew up. I do not think my brother knew exactly, outside of being a cattle rustler or the commander of a blockade runner, of which we'd seen no job openings for around town. I wasn't sure what exact career I wanted either, but it had to involve the adult equivalent of putting all the pieces of an erector set the dog knocked over back together while fending off bad guys with my plastic six shooter (and maybe a G.I. Joe helicopter).

We'd talk as the sun set, watching permutations of light through the trees darken in the ground's acceptance as we huddled in hazy camouflage. We talked until silence blew across our dreams, and only the sound of an owl rippled the surface of the water, the smell of the pine trees on our face. We'd sleep the dreamless sleep of children, waking up under the clumped mirage of trees, to the distant bugle of an elk, the reveille of the wild. Those starry nights kept us going as future days grew darker.

Dreams are often interrupted by startling noise, by shifts in light and shadow, by the very whoosh of the blood in our veins. Ours were interrupted by a long and eventually terminal battle of my Mom with cancer. With Dad lost in the grief of Mom's fate and Big Bro off in the Navy, under the ocean in places he would never reveal, not even to me, I spent a lot of time just out walking, out into the tree line near home, trying to figure out what I wanted to do with myself when I grew up.

There in those woods one day, under a thick canopy of trees, I stumbled across a small and very dead, female whitetail deer. There were no visible marks of violence upon that little Jane Doe. It looked as if she just lay down, waiting for death to catch up. She had been dead a while, perhaps a week, exposed to wind and air and warmth; the breakdown of the flesh to bone does not take long. I was surprised that scavengers hadn't been at her, but under cover, this close to the lights of a house, in a spring ripe with things to eat; she had been spared further insult.

Yet, unlike humans, this once breathing creature had no one that would miss her, death being simply a breakdown of the body, not a function of the mind and the heart and all the bereavement it can contain. I looked at her form and I did not think of God or the Devil playing a hand in what brought her here, but rather a primitive force that existed long before good and evil. Death. Atheists believe that a death is the end, after that, simply darkness. Those who believe in the Divine believe it is a beginning; a journey home to glory. But that day, I stood there and simply wondered how that journey started, what brought her to this fate, and how I could have prevented it. It was then I think I realized what would be my life's passion when I grew up, perhaps one day a vocation, and how I would travel to get there.

I pursued it with single vision. I'd started taking summer college classes at fourteen years old, but now I had a focus as to what I wanted to do with it. All the basic academics behind me, I went full speed into it, not letting anyone get near me or close to where that grief lived and grew. Until I met someone, older, charming, promising me more stars than would fit in the dark, cool liquid of the night, hinting at the promise of family that I no longer seemed to have. Sometimes we are so focused on the dream, there is no room in our souls for gratitude or caution. I ended up pregnant, discarded the moment I disclosed it, our lives removed from his with a quick, cold precision of a surgical blade. I was eighteen years old.

A few months later, I gave birth after thirty long hours. I saw her only once, held up above the bloody sheets. At ten pounds, six ounces, she was hard to miss, with soft reddish blond hair and my rosy cheeks. Then, before I could touch her, she was whisked away, her new parents anxious to meet her and finalize the adoption.

The delivery, being difficult, kept me there a couple of days in that quiet Catholic hospital. They put me on the floor away from the new mothers. Still the occasional nurse, outside of required medical checks, and more than one nun stopped by to give me a smile and a gentle touch on the arm. They looked at me with eyes that had likely witnessed all the cruelty and pain of the world, yet filled with a vision of a place that knows not sin, but rather forgiveness. They were nothing but kind. We did not talk. I did not cry.

Dad took me home and tucked me into my bed. It was the New Year, and with the bitter cold outside, the window had to stay shut. As I lay there in the dark, realized I could no longer smell the trees. The tears finally came.

My life did not go exactly as planned; the profession I was interested in took a detour while I spent more than a few years in a swept wing jet that went faster than my Mom would have approved of. In that time there was a marriage, not the joy I had hoped for, but simply a place where some dreams went to die, there was aloneness, and there were dogs, but none that truly were my own.

Finally, now, wings hung up, with a well paying job more fitting with my childhood dreams and a big, new house being purchased soon, just for me, it was time.

It was time for a black lab, one that I'd picked out from a litter in a small town in the Eastern United States. A black lab, still not big enough to come home with me, who would be given the name of Barkley.

I call and tell my Dad the news. Instead of a lecture, I just hear the smile in his voice as he says, "I wish your Mom could see the two of you." When he speaks of her, his eyes still gleam oh-so-suddenly-and-bright, like a kerosene lamp does just before the flame goes dark. He loved her through more than thirty years, through hunger and abundance, through two rounds of cancer. He loved her without fail, just as he's loved me through stubbornness, defiance and choices he'd rather have given his life for, than to watch me reap the consequences. But he was not the sort to protect me to the point of not letting me learn of consequences.

And he never said, "I told you so" as I chased my dreams - the ones he smiles and shakes his head at now, the ones that brought me deep satisfaction, the ones that caused me deep hurt. For he understands that inborn desire to shield the innocence from which we are born and by which we embrace our choices, trusting and wide eyed, carrying some through more than one skirmish that brings with it scars, carrying at least one with us, furiously home again, to glory.

I open the door to go pick up my puppy, heading out to the car, the smell of the trees on the air.

3

Homecomings

The drive to Barkley's home was a long one, and I took a friend so that one of us could drive, and one could hold him on the way home. I could have found a black lab closer to home, but a colleague owned a female from a previous litter and she was such a great dog that when I heard there was going to be another litter I made sure I let them know I wanted one. I was also told I could have first pick of the litter after his family selected one. Barkley's father was a National Grand Field Champion. His mom was purebred but was simply someone's beloved pet, not a show dog. He came from good, healthy stock and I was so excited to finally bring him home.

I'd selected him a few weeks prior, but he would not be released to me until he was a bit bigger, and had socialized. When I arrived that first day, there were eight puppies all tumbling on the ground like flightless bumblebees, all looking almost identical, but for one larger puppy that the owners were keeping and naming Bear.

So cute, but how do I pick? Some of them came frolicking

over to me, mindlessly entertained by the smell of new shoes. Barkley just sat and looked at me, as intent as I've seen in a puppy. It was a look of hesitation, not through fear, not physically, but in his little doggy spirit, that profoundly sober alertness you see in someone of quiet intelligence as they size you up.

After assessing me carefully, he came over and sniffed my hand, then sat at my feet, ignoring the other people there with me, snuffling at my shoelaces while the other pups, losing interest, went off to chase a bug or something. Barkley didn't leave me the rest of the time I was there. Where I went, he went and simply sat and looked at me with satisfaction.

There was a moment of hesitation on my part. Yes, this had been a dream of mine for a long time, but I'd already lost my Mom. Did I want to open myself up for loss again? Their lifespan is so short and my heart still aches when I thought about the loss of the last family pet, even if, my being gone so much, we didn't have a close bond.

But this was now. He was so small, and at that moment we both felt like we could live forever, me in my excitement, he in his somber evaluation of me that said either, "Yes, you're going to be my Mom" or "Look lady, you are too old to be wearing Daisy Duke Shorts."

My friend and I got him loaded up, my friend driving, Barkley and I in the front where I could hold him firmly. I was worried he might be upset by the separation from his "family" but when I came for him, he was just sitting there with an obedient air, as if he'd been expecting this very moment. Little did I know, the "obedience" was just a clever ruse until he wormed his way into my heart.

We figured we'd be home in an hour until that first dead traffic light, then another, then another all ceasing to work. Was the whole neighborhood out? We turned on the radio. Apparently most of the Eastern Seaboard was out. It was a giant power grid failure that blacked out most of the state, and several others.

I knew back roads with more stop signs and fewer traffic lights, and we headed out that way, but it still took four hours to make that drive. My friend left to check on his family, and Barkley happily did his business on my tiny lawn and followed me to the porch.

He refused to go inside.

I know, it's scary for him, and it's dark inside. I picked him up and carried him in, giving him a little nibble of a treat and some water, still holding him, as I opened blinds up so he could see his new home.

The power was off all night, but we were OK. I cooked burgers out on the barbecue, and with a breeze blowing off one of the Great Lakes, we were reasonably cool, even those of us wearing fur coats.

With the house in darkness but for a camping lantern and

candles, and good ventilation from outside, I just decided to go to bed early. I put him in his crate, all fixed up with a soft shirt inside that I'd worn so it would smell familiar, and I climbed into bed. The window was cracked open; the only sound was the soft silver tinkle of glasses, as the neighbors cleaned up from their impromptu cookout in the shared drive. A flash of faded light broke the space between us, not the power coming back on, just someone's headlights, and he stirred with a gentle cry.

There was no ignoring that sound, a plaintive little cry of loneliness, the anguish of a helpless creature who doesn't understand what he so terribly misses. He'd never slept in a crate, always with his Mom and brothers and sisters.

I wasn't sure exactly what to do; it had been a long, long while since I was around a puppy, and I wasn't sure exactly what he needed. Food, water, go outside? What is it when we grapple with our pet's innate needs, and we perceive how congruent and consistent they are, those canine companions with which we share a future, a home, and all the stars above it? They just want to be safe and be loved, no different from us.

I got up, opened his crate and picked him up. I lay down on the sofa, Barkley on my chest, nuzzled up to something making him think "well, these don't come with food, but they are soft" and went contentedly to sleep.

It took him a moment to size me up before he selected me, but this first night together, his little doggie heart beating against mine and his tongue licking my cheek, I was the one tasting the finiteness of life, and the inestimable chance we have to connect and love again.

Some things are just too precious to pass up even as we know we can't hold them forever.

4

Behold a Horse

Barkley soon settled into the routine of my little household, although those first couple of weeks of getting up during the night to take him outside, sometimes more than once, was wearing on me. I knew that soon though, he'd be able to sleep through the night.

When I went to bed tonight, after a busy week, I was hoping that tonight would be one of those nights.

Severe thunderstorms had been stalking the area. After listening to the old fashioned stereo for a while, I went to bed, leaving it on, noticing the light on the console near the bed but deciding just to roll over and sleep. About two o'clock in the morning, the power went out, and then came back on immediately. Then there was a small click sound, the drawer with the CD in it opening and closing, played on the cold air. The sound, unusual in my sleep, brought me up from a deep slumber, but just barely. As the ground shook and the sky boomed, the bedroom windows lit up with lightning. My eyes still closed, I was not yet aware of where I was, the sleep still lingering. Then a deep voice filled the room.

> "And I heard as it were
> the noise of thunder
> One of the four beasts saying come and see
> and I saw
> And behold a white horse"

From my somnolent state all I could think was "It's GOD, and He sounds just like Johnny Cash!"

Some voices just stay with you, for you to recall in an instant, a memory.

But the voices we really remember come with memories of more than the TV set, but times and places in our lives. One such memory was a favorite science teacher in high school, his voice competing with the clatter and clink of glass, the hoarse cough of the Bunsen burners and the animated chatter of aspiring geeks, his voice a calm direction among chaos, as we attempted to blow the whole experiment up.

Being teens, we tended to ignore him. Yet it was his voice I heard, years later, exhausted from two jobs and college, poring over books that I read not so much in that I wanted to read them, but knew that I must. For I was too aware that I must somehow absorb the words in these brief evening hours, measuring the turning pages against the fleeing strokes of irreversible time, ticking with the measured precision of that library clock.

It's not just voices you remember, it is sounds.

I remember Christmas Eve as a small child. I'd sleep on a folding cot that was placed next to my big brother's bed. Mom would tuck us both in while Dad went to "do some last minute chores" (probably cursing up a storm during the assembly of the Barbie Dream House). We'd lie there in the dark, my brother, from his grown up bed, speaking to his little sister in that soft whisper of childhood, under the glow of big 1960s Christmas lights outside the window. We'd left cookies and milk out for Santa though Dad suggested he'd prefer pretzels and a beer. Then we tried to stay awake as long as we could, hoping to hear Santa's arrival.

The clock ticked later and later, the house quiet. "Do you hear it?" Big Bro would quietly exclaim. But the clattering sound we heard was not reindeer on the roof, but the dog's toenails on the hardwood floor as she patrolled the hall, checking on her two legged pups.

So many sounds we remember. I remember the sound of bat meeting ball as I played with him out in the yard. The CRACK as aerodynamics and physics greet one another, the ball just a spherical dream of speed heading out into the trees as the dog raced to recover it before we did. I remember the sound of the piano, as I practiced hour after hour as a child. Beethoven, Bach, Debussy. The sounds of the music filled the house, filling me, the opening chords of Rhapsody in Blue awakening something in me I was too naive to articulate.

I remember the sound of taps played at a funeral of someone I cherished, the wreckage of duty crashing on the ears of those who are left. But it was a sound that fell without lasting damage for we were raised to be fighters, stronger than wreckage, taller than fear. Honor the fallen and continue the fight.

The thunderstorms tonight still fill the sky with their own sound show. The stereo turned off, I hear the click of Barkley's little puppy toenails on the hardwood floor of the hall, a steadily measured sound, as strangely comforting as a clock. He settles down on his little bed by mine, happily able to sleep through the night without going outside and happy to be free of the crate.

I look at a folded flag there atop the dresser; I listen to a house that has been empty for such a long while.

I almost wish he'd wake me to go out just so I could hold him for a moment. But with a smile, I roll over and go back to sleep.

5

Would You Like a Wakeup Call?

It was the cold nose that woke me up, pushing up against my hand with no small insistence. Barkley was sleeping through the night now, nudging my hand or nudging the little bell on the front door if he needed to go out. This morning was too early. Apparently his great canine instinct detected that this was Mom's day off, so he'd best get her up early.

Normally, I only get up early on purpose for work or bird hunting trips. On such days, I wake while the sky is black infinitude. As I leave the house there is only a small sliver of moonlight to guide, a moonbeam's soft caress sculpting my form as I hike up a hill, as if climbing closer to the sky, I can hold heaven even closer.

Even on work days, I love to watch the color of the dawn, as it turns from black to pink to orange to the brilliant white of the world. When the dawn lightens behind the stark shapes of your life, and like a rose unfolding, like a lover's first kiss, there's a quivering beginning of hope that can't be deterred, even with bad coffee, and an early meeting.

Today, I do not want to see the dawn, a pheasant or anything, but the inside of my eyelids, snuggled face down, legs extended, arms out, laid out upon the still warm bed. But I know that eventually, I will have to get up. But today is Saturday. Today I do not want to. I'm not exhausted but neither am I bound by some duty to leap out of bed, I'm simply hung up in a limb of time beneath a sullen night sky that will continue to wane toward yet another morning until I voluntarily release my grip, falling toward the earth. In the meantime, it does not matter because there's no one waiting for me to get up.

Well, there is no one except him. So with soft warm breath and the nudge of whiskers he finds me, underneath the warm blanket, as an usher would gently nudge a soul found napping in a pew after services are over, helping me toward the door with the urgency born of prisoned energy and small doggie bladder.

We've been walking two to three miles each morning after breakfast, and again after work, waiting for the time we can move into our new house with a yard. There is also a tennis court on site, fenced and usually empty so he can play in it with me without a leash. Barkley will run and grab that tennis ball, like a pro, except the part where he lobs it back. Barkley has not yet learned the "give it up" part of retrieving.

I tried to talk myself into the six miles a day of walking by telling myself I'd lose weight. After many weeks and many more miles, I found I'd gained two pounds, likely due to my tired brain not being able to differentiate between an orange and a candy bar after getting up three times during the night to let him out. Why did I imagine I need a dog, I'd think as my feet hit the cold floor yet again, the wind outside a portent to only one color, and that is a frozen blue.

"Barkley, at least you have a fur coat," I tell him as I layer myself up to go out.

But there's something uplifting in watching him head out, this small complex of townhomes his entire world, as he orbits me yet again, in a circle, wrapping me up in his leash, caught in the gravity of his "person." "OK, Barkley, let's get us untangled and we'll go."

We step out the door; the sky comes alive with deep royal tones that in centuries past would have been worn by only the most privileged. The horizon blooms with the lush yellow and deep purple of ripe fruit, taste and texture against the plate of the earth that pales to gold and then soft blue, the colors of the sky I remember from my last time aloft, colors I hope I never forget. I close my eyes with an internal "click" as I capture them all in all the film of memory as Barkley I leave the house, the landscape brimming with the promise of light.

6

Run Away!

Barkley and I had established a routine. I'd walk him before work and after work, as well. I had a dog sitter/walker, a retired nurse who had a licensed business for just such a purpose and who loved Barkley as her own. She took him out twice a day for playtime and a walk when I was working.

We were working on basic commands; still, I had to keep an eye on him as he didn't always come when I called. I had closed on my new house and I wanted him to be close by and obeying me when we moved in, as I did not have a fence for it yet, having to get permission from the homeowners' association after moving.

This morning, I was up early, the complex quiet. I had the garage door open for just a moment to maneuver a trash barrel out, Barkley playing with a toy inside the kitchen, the door ajar. Suddenly there came this enormous BOOM of noise from a distance. I had no idea what it was, though it came from the direction of a coal/steam/power plant of some sort I knew was nearby. BOOM!

Barkley was out the door into the garage and out of the garage like a shot, running for his life.

"Barkley, come back!" I cried, but with yet another BOOM, he continued on, terrified.

My little townhouse is far back from the main road into the complex, still I run hard to try and lure him in, dressed in my flannel pajama bottoms and a sweatshirt. The more I move toward him, the further away he runs, toward not just the entrance but the busy road from which it comes.

"Barkley, come here. *Treat, Treat, Treat, Treat!*"

For just a moment, I totally regret this whole dog thing. I could be sitting in my house, sipping coffee, having a croissant, the picture of a successful professional getting ready for work, but no, I'm running down the road like a mad woman in Bugs Bunny pajama bottoms.

I could have gotten a cat. No, I'm not a cat person. I could have got a pet rock. Or a BMW.

"Barkley!"

But you cannot put a value on a living creature anymore than you can give a measure to everything that has weight. Some things you are just bound to discover, there in a house where you've been locked away too long, or simply breathing, there in the moment of time you shared on a small planet spinning in space, destined to meet.

"Barkley!" I'm getting mad now as he surges ahead, his months-old puppy legs faster than I can run in slippers. BOOM, the sound comes again. He's heading straight for the main road.

I can only describe it like that moment in the movie Jaws, where the camera looms in on Sheriff Brody, and the whole world focuses. It does, for just a moment. You suddenly notice every little detail around you, the sun running straight and empty, like a gash through the street, a tiny spider web there at the edge of your vision, hanging from a tree, the sun piercing it, illuminating the space there between the delicate strength. I no longer feel annoyance, but the potential of loss, not just an animal, but my friend, held at that moment with conviction, that sense, that feeling of home.

There's no way I'm going to let him get to the main road, where traffic is busy. If he will just stop, I can catch up, but as I approach, he just runs further away, still scared. I cut over, behind a few homes, hoping to jump ahead where he cannot sense me chasing him and might slow or stop, to "cut him off at the pass." I didn't know I could run this hard in slippers, even more importantly; I didn't know I could jump for I went over a kid's little lawn chair behind someone's back patio like it was a hurdle from my high school track days.

Sometimes you do not know what you have in you until something you love is threatened. Then you simply reach down to the core of your reserve, which occurs at intervals in all of us, driving us to lay down the known and the safe, to seek possession of something that has been long lost to us, blind to everything but hope and fate.

Dear Lord, I hope no one is looking

There, I'm in front of him, and he turns back toward the house, still running, but tiring, and calming, the loud sound ceasing.

I catch up and scoop him up in my arms. He's still trembling; the noise stopped. Apparently, the power plant was letting off some steam or something. The neighbor's said they had heard that before.

That night, I let him sleep upon the bed with me. That probably doesn't help with the "No; I'm the alpha dog" thing, but tonight I do not care.

We lie there, the upstairs window open to the stars, and it is like lying out in a tent with my brother as kids, where we'd rest, unable to sleep, listening to the night's whisper, talking of our past adventures. The past is our future, but we couldn't taste that, until it too was our past. Everything else is illusion.

Except this warm bundle of fur sleeping peacefully next to me.

7

Getting Skunked Is Not Just for Cribbage

We'd finally moved to the newly constructed house. It was located only a block or so from where my rental unit was so Barkley and I walked over to it and around it a couple of times a day. I hoped that would make the transition to living there an easy one for a young dog. I was looking forward to it. It had lots of space for me, not needed really, but it seemed everyone was buying homes out in the fancier subdivisions, so I figured it was time for that move. Besides, Barkley needed a yard. The yard was a lot smaller than I expected given the cost of the home, but there was about thirty acres of woods behind (future subdivision) with an assortment of gentle critters that made for a nice view.

We'd been in it a couple of months when one night, Barkley begins growling and barking at the door. I figure it is his arch enemy, the squirrel, so I let him out to the newly fenced yard and he goes running out back toward the edge of the woods, barking fiercely. This isn't a squirrel, which he barks at almost with laughter, but something bigger and unknown to him. Something he perceived as a real threat.

He could have stayed in the house; he could have barked a warning and come on in. But there was something out there that was nothing he'd seen before and he was going to go after it, to find out that it just takes two to postulate the certainties of being outgunned.

He charged at the darkness with no fear and no quarter, only to get sprayed by the neighborhood equivalent of a weapon of mass destruction, a big skunk.

Fortunately his enemy's aim was off and he didn't get it in the face, but Barkley was still seriously stinky--enough to make us both tear up. I called a friend who has several dogs to see what I should do. I'd heard that using tomato juice will get rid of the smell. After his wife quit laughing, they told me not to use tomato juice to get rid of the smell but to use something that works much better. Well, there's just no politically correct way to say this but they suggested I use feminine hygiene douche. Apparently I guess it works real well on . . . well, you get my drift.

So I put Barkley in the bathroom and made the dash to CVS about nine in the evening to buy about twenty boxes of the stuff, enough to add to a little water to give him a bath in the tub. The girl at the counter was looking at all the boxes, then at me, and a strange puzzled look appeared on her face. She said, "Uh - my, you're certainly buying a lot of this tonight?"

Of course, by way of explanation I said quite cheerily. . . . ."Oh, it's for my dog."

She couldn't get me out of the store fast enough.

Barkley took his "bath" and almost smelled, well, "springtime fresh." Almost. But not enough to where I wanted him on his bed in my room, so I put him in the basement, in a bigger crate I'd purchased for him, on a nest of an old, comfy, washable bedspread. I then went up two flights of stairs, took a shower and fell into bed. After about fifteen minutes of lights out, I heard the gentle whine coming up through the heating ducts, that dearth-like moan of loneliness. So despite a smell that could only be described as "Eau de French Brothel," I let Barkley upstairs. He was damp and still a bit in shock, but he promptly settled down on the carpeting, where he could guard the bedroom door in case the skunk had learned to pick a lock.

I didn't mind. After all, he took the blast from the skunk simply trying to protect me and his home from an intruder. Frankly, he would have gone up against a grizzly to protect me, without hesitating about it, weighing the options or thinking "what's in this for me?" If need be, he would have written with his life his own final footnote while I sat inside reading dusty chronicles of the past, unaware of his sacrifice. All he asked in return was love and my company, all that he needed to assuage his heart's thirst.

The next evening I sat at my computer, a mug of tea nearby. As I thought about the previous evening it really sank in. Those that truly love us, do so as we are, without expectations or demands. They forgive human frailty; they embrace our joys and they share the sorrows. I have had friends like that. I have a dog like that. Dogs are simple. Give them your loyalty and affection and they will give you theirs. Sometimes it takes nothing more than a bout with Pepe' Le Pew to remind me of all that they do for us and how lucky we are to have them.

But I'll probably avoid that CVS for a while.

8

When Life Gives you Lemons

I was quickly discovering that Barkley, like most labs, will eat most anything. But Barkley seemed to have a more sensitive stomach than other labs I have known, not doing well with cheap dog food or even small bits of people food. More than once in his first year of life, I came into the room to find a chagrined pooch and a pile of dog barf off in a corner.

The vet could find nothing to worry about, but we did switch him to a higher quality dog food and treats and the only "people food" he was going to get would be the rare treat of a nibble of unseasoned cooked meat and frozen veggies. I checked which ones are safe for dogs and he tried several of them in tiny, treat sized quantities Brussels sprouts (they're all yours, buddy), peas, and carrots (Spew! Spew!). OK, he didn't much like the carrots.

He still tried for people food; I just learned to be careful.

It started one night when Barkley and I were staying with a friend who lived out in the country for a weekend. The first night, she got called into work, so it was just the two of us and I had a craving for pizza. The town was pretty much a stoplight, so the only pizza was at a convenience store, but it was pretty good--made fresh there. It was a long drive, and it was late, but after making sure the house was "Barkley Proof," I left him to retrieve a small personal-sized one.

I'd returned to the house, and gotten a plate and beverage, when I realized I needed to go wash up first. Setting the pizza down, I went into the bathroom. When I emerged just a couple of minutes later, the pizza was gone. Barkley was curled up on the floor sound asleep. "What?" Maybe I just thought I set it on the table, I might have set it in on the counter in the kitchen.

Suddenly, Barkley let out this enormous *belch*, filling the room with pepperoni fumes.

That's the last time I left him alone with a pizza.

Still, those begging eyes are hard to deal with, and he'll beg for anything, beer, a cough drop, toothpaste. If it smells like food, he wants some.

Tonight, back at our own house, he was begging for a slice of lemon that I was slicing to make a meringue pie.

"Dude, its lemon, you're *not* going to like it."

He persisted. I checked first the list of foods you should never give a dog, and didn't see lemon there, only their seeds. I gave him a small slice, without the rind, carefully checking all seeds were removed. He ran into the dining room with his prize.

I went to watch, to see if he'd really eat it.

He chewed. His face scrunched up, his eyes squeezed shut; he shook himself once and slowly swallowed with a small whine. That lemon slice did *not* go down easy.

Then, I swear he was smiling. The tail was wagging. He was snooting my hand. He wanted *another* piece! He looked at me as if to say "Mom, it's so horrendously bad it's good, like that movie we watched with the fat, aging action hero."

But I could not be surprised; this was a dog that had eaten a paper napkin, a worm and an entire pizza all with the same enthusiasm. He was also a dog that sat by the edge of the kitchen table because a small meat loaf had accidentally been knocked off it to be immediately "retrieved."

Even after it was devoured, he sat there in the crop circle of barbecue sauce stain on the floor for an hour, waiting for the mother ship to drop another chunk of beef to earth.

"Sorry, Barkley, no more people food for you," I said as I added kibble to his food bowl. The bowl sat on a mat that has two circles marked on them, one labeled "water," the other "nasty dry crap."

To make him feel better, I had a rice cake for dinner.

9

Driving Lessons

It was time to get Barkley acclimated to the vehicle. He had done one short ride to the vet for a checkup and booster shots, and went with me to a girlfriend's house a couple of months ago. But both trips were made when he was totally worn out from play, so he did not fuss too much as I hooked him into a makeshift harness in the back seat that would keep him secure.

How to contain him as he grew was an issue. He was growing rapidly; his paws giving me an idea, that when fully grown, he was going to be eighty pounds or more. The front seat was out of the question, as the air bag could kill him. My little car had a fairly small back seat, but for now, he could lay out comfortably on it.

But I was getting out in the community and driving more than just to work: attending community events I'd never gone to before, exploring new parks, places that he could travel to. With no family in this state, I sometimes even made the drive out to the West Coast, a long trip he might enjoy in the future. I do not mind the drive, a multi-day trip but still cheaper than flying. I like to drive and sometimes just head out in my vehicle, with no intended destination, just to explore the roads.

What I remember distinctly from childhood is "going out for a drive." Does anyone just "go out for a drive" in these days of high priced gasoline? When was the last time you got into your car or truck with no real plan as to where the day would take you? Driving simply to drive, not maneuvering from Point A to Point B while also doing other things but simply heading to where the sky slaps the horizon line. No phones, no TV for anyone in the back seat, no teleconference. Sure the radio might be on sometimes, but you do not need to send a fax at the same time. It seems as if everyone in a car anymore has to multi-task. Talking on the phone, eating, drinking, reading the newspaper (yes), putting on makeup, usually while the rest of us are slamming on the brakes, cursing and giving them the "you're #1" hand signal.

As kids, we'd pile into the old station wagon every summer and drive to the Southwest, my aunt and uncle's small ranch several states away. While we were there, our folks would relax and joke and listen to music that I listen to today. We would play with our cousins outside all day: tossing stones up at bats flitting through night trees, watching them swoop down, swimming in the irrigation ditches, riding a small motorbike around. But as fun as that was, what I remember most is the drive to get there. As kids, Big Bro and I got along, but there was the occasional "Mom! They're on *my* side" when someone was tired and cranky, as Dad threatened to pull over at least once, as has every father in recorded history.

We saw much on those trips--great dams to which jeweled fish leaped, old forts in which we could almost hear the volley of weapons, the shadows of men on a ground they had long since quitted. We saw our Mom, even then going through that first round of chemo, turning her face up to the sun, reaching up for each last bit of life.

We had no videos; we had no computerized toys, and in the early years, we had no air conditioning. But there would always be a moment a few hours into the trip, where already merged onto the road, we would merge into a family again. On today's drive, I would not have my Big Bro with me, but I would have my furry best friend. He could join me on a drive, that journey becoming a game, matching wits against the elements and the curve of asphalt, weathered buildings, outcroppings of soil and rock, cars and trains that move past the window in a diorama of color and speed.

To Barkley it was just going to be new smells and fresh air. To me it was an open road, a dimension free of time and space that flows from childhood to the hazy secret door to the future. It's a road little changed from a child's hand out the window in the breeze to the older foot on the gas pedal, pressing down, carrying with it the echo of childish want, the passion and unrest of adulthood. The road rushes under me, rushing on, way too quickly.

Where did this last year go? Barkley was growing up so quickly. It was time to get him set to make a trip home with me someday, so he too could enjoy sights and smells of the roads. But

I needed to find something sturdier than what I had used a couple of times to keep him from flying forward in an accident, something that would hook onto his harness with the attach point at his upper shoulders.

The harness was not something he liked. Even with training he still pulled way too hard on the leash when he was excited but I would never use a choke collar on him--most of them looking like something a teen punk rock fan might have worn in the 80's, much to their parent's dismay.

The harness had soft padded front loops that would gently bind his front legs without pain, if he pulled too hard, which would work with the leash. It would also work with a connection device to attach him to the seat belt, though it was sometimes time consuming to put on.

The first time he looked at me like it was some torture device.

"Barkley, it's no worse than an underwire bra, and trust me, sometimes you just need to wear it."

He ran, he hid, and he grabbed my slippers, anything to get out of putting the harness on. I finally got him to sit, gave him a treat, and placed it over his head, the "sit" for a treat, worth it for a moment to him. I then got him to "shake," slipping the front loop of cord and fabric over one foot, then the other. He's in!

Today, we went through the same routine, but he finally sat

and allowed it to be placed on him, realizing that until he did, we were not going "out." It then attached to a new device I found that locked into the seatbelt. He could then sit or lie down, but he would not fly forward in a sudden stop as "the amazing projectile dog!"

It was time for a test drive. Just a short one through the country, where traffic would be light, and he wouldn't be alarmed by unusual sound, horns or traffic. I got a few big bone shaped dog treats in a small plastic container, should I need to reward or bribe him, a dog dish, a big jug of water and an emergency bacon sandwich, because, sometimes you just need emergency bacon.

Remember how I said I did not like to multi-task? I like sitting still even less. Just like a little kid, I tend to get restless when the ride comes to a stop.

For there I am, on a lonely country road, waiting for a slow moving piece of farm machinery to cross the intersecting road. I have no big brother to annoy, and even Barkley is starting to look bored.

I looked out onto the land. The soil was shallow here. Digging down, one finds rock too soon. Things do not stay buried long, finding a way of working themselves to the surface, like acorns of autumns past, struggling up toward the light, to the scoured sky of a glittering sun, to the promise of life.

I smile and reach down to crank up the stereo. LaBelle is the first song up on this oldie's music channel. The windows of the vehicle are down to a beautiful late summer afternoon, no one else on this four lane stretch of road. I crank *up* the volume even more.

Gitchi Gitchi Ya Ya Ta Ta
Gitchi Gitchi Ya Ya Here
Mocha choca lata Ya Ya
Creole Lady Marmalade

Voulez-vous coucher avec moi, ce soir?
Voulez-vous coucher avec moi?

And yes, I was singing along, loudly, using a big dog biscuit as a microphone, shaking my red hair around. Barkley was barking along to the chorus, "Woof! Woof!" when I glanced out of the corner of my eye, and there next to me, waiting as well, was an eighty-year-old man in an old truck giving me a *big* wink and thumbs up before turning right.

There was one downfall to coming out of your solitary shell and getting out into the community again. Someone from the American Legion Pancake Breakfast next month was going to point toward me and tell a friend a story about a crazy woman singing into a dog biscuit.

10

I've Got My Animal, Where's My Ark?

I woke to the sound of rain outside. It had been pouring for days, it seemed. Barkley and I had resorted to throwing a ball around the unfinished basement to get a little exercise during the day as even he did not want to go out in a heavy downpour other than for essential business.

Normally, I enjoy it when it rains like this. But when you're alone, it is different. It seems like time drapes across your senses, the water and the wind drowning out more than the light. It is a heightened state of awareness that is the first kiss of perception. There was a lot I needed to do on this place outside, the new landscaping, almost a full time job. But then came the rain, each and every morning, all week and those tasks just seemed to diminish in the background of it. There was nothing I could do but settle back, realizing nothing was going to happen soon, no matter how much I wished it would. Anticipation is the best part of anything and the rain only whets the desire to see the sunshine again.

We'd been in the house for a while now, but I was starting to regret buying such a big place. I had saved for years to buy it, living very modestly so I could put a huge down payment on it. So my monthly payment was manageable, but it seemed like every time I turned around, there was an expense. Sure, there was a "how much do you charge for just one room" carpet cleaning, for Barkley had to be the barfiest dog I'd ever had. The vet found nothing wrong; he was healthy and eating a good dog food. Once we kept him away from some greasier people food that folks would give as "treats" it lessened considerably, but he sometimes still left me a "surprise." It was usually because he wolfed down his food like I had not fed him in days, and then up it came.

I'd started just feeding him half the amount, enduring the "I'm going to call the SPCA right now" stare, and then giving him the other half, fifteen minutes later. That seemed to do the trick. But occasionally, he'd still eat too fast, and it would happen again.

After the pizza incident, I was incredibly diligent about not leaving food around. At two years old now, Barkley was big enough to reach things higher up.

This Saturday, it was still pouring, even after taking him out on the leash briefly in the yard. I'd been up late, a date--someone I'd met at a community gathering of like minded folks. After chatting online, we had a couple of meetings for coffee. Finally, I invited him over for lunch at my house, and then we were going to a small concert at the park.

Barkley did not seem too taken with him, which surprised me, as he loves everyone; but my date made a feeble attempt to pat him. The lunch went well, even with a grumpy dog, but as we were getting ready to leave and he leaned in as if to kiss me, his phone rang. I could hear some woman, obviously upset about something in her day. I could not hear every word of what she was saying, as she was not just loud, but agitated, but I understood the words "our wedding next month."

He'd failed to mention a fiancée.

That was the world's shortest date. Well, not exactly. There was that blind date someone set me up with. Unknown to me, he was a white collar criminal with an ankle bracelet who thought LEO was my astrological sign, not my profession. After he asked who I worked for, and I told him, he was out the door before the appetizers and our steaks arrived, leaving me with a check at an ultra-expensive restaurant *and* no ride home.

As I went to bed tonight, the sky weeping outside, I thought about that, the possibility of becoming a nun at my age, or even calling up that old boyfriend I'd broken up with some time back because he was much more serious than I, wanting to get married and have kids and my reaction was "Run Away! Run Away." That's in the past. It needed to stay in the past. It was the right decision for me, even if I was left alone with the breathing of rain and the cold that surrounds it; nothing behind or ahead, it seems, but the heavy heartbeat of silence you never conceive of when you're young.

The next morning, it was still raining. Although the backyard was fenced, it had some very wet and muddy spots in it, so I took Barkley out with boots and leash to keep him away from those areas. As raindrops dripped from a tree branch, I touched my tongue to my lips, tasting salt. The air had gone cold, wind stroking with a touch that's neither caress nor dismissal. So, my house was too much work and my social life stank; at least pancakes would make me feel better.

Barkley settled back on his dog bed downstairs and went back to sleep, surprisingly uninterested in my cooking activities. "That's odd," I thought, as usually, he was practically glued to my side as I prepared food.

The pancakes made, I set them on the table and started to eat.

Suddenly, Barkley jumped up and ran to the door with that "I have to go! I have to go *now*!" dance that was becoming familiar. The leash was handy, but I'd put my boots out in the garage as they were wet.

"Hang on, Barkley," I said as I went out into the garage to get my boots.

I came back in and he was curled up on his bed, no longer having to go, and not having an accident that I could see as I looked around the room.

My pancakes, however, were missing.

I'd been set up.

I did not think the weekend could get much worse. Then from the basement, I heard the sound of water. I heard the little sump pump; it had been going non-stop for three days now. But there was a new, unfamiliar sound.

I turned on the light and headed down the stairs to find my basement completely flooded with about four inches of water.

Barkley followed me, fueled by pancakes and bounded down the steps, splashing right into it as if saying. "Mom, you made me a pond! Thanks!"

It was going to be one of those days.

11

Soldiers In Your Cup

Ow! Ow! Ow!

It was six o'clock in the morning and I had just gotten up to brew a pot of coffee when I stubbed my toe on yet another hard rubber dog toy.

Where did that come from?

When I went to bed, Barkley was lying on the middle landing on the stairs, where the sun warms the carpet up before dark and from which he can survey the front door. His toys were all down the hall in my office where he hangs out with me in the evening when I'm on the computer.

But apparently during the night, he brought his toys into my bedroom, additional reinforcements perhaps for the protection of "Mom."

His toys had evolved since he was a puppy. When he was little he had a big goofy looking squeaky spider and a plush elephant that he carried around in his mouth constantly, never chewing on them, just toting them around and even sleeping with them. Somewhere in the growing process, however, he decided toys were better chewed on than used as play toys.

Soft or thin rubber toys were de-squeaked within minutes of presentation, the happiest minutes of his life by his own accord. I would hear “squeak squeak squeak” to the point I was contemplating grabbing hearing protection from my range bag, then suddenly, silence. I’d look over at him sitting there with the squeaky device lying on the carpet surrounded by tufts of stuffing and shredded fabric. Given what some of the fancier toys cost and how quickly he destroyed them, I figured even Congress could not spend money like that, in such a time frame.

I could occasionally find a super cheap stuffed animal on sale for a buck that I would give him, knowing it would be destroyed. I even found on sale a high quality stuffed duck that also squeaked (likely due to the duck having a pneumothorax). I thought with the sturdier materials it might at least last a few days. But it also only lasted a few minutes, and I was growing concerned that he might accidentally swallow parts of the toys, even if he never tried to. Future toys were going to be tooth proof.

It’s tough for me to remember he’s a dog, not able to understand “that would *not* be smart to eat.” For I grew up in a generation that still had toys that heated up, could blow up, or leave scars.

Think about it, why can't you get the kids a good old Sonic Blaster anymore? Nothing like a toy that perforates the eardrums the old fashioned way, they used to say. Blame it on the Cold War or the TV show The Man from UNCLE, but in the last part of the sixties, when I was small, we had some of the best toys. They would be considered by some to be dangerous, life threatening toys but they put the BOOM in baby boomer. The sonic blaster was one of the best, a pump-action gun that fired a big column of air toward distant enemies of the state. Sit in a room full of middle aged men and say "Sonic Blaster" and I guarantee at least three guys will smile and go "FOOOOMMM! We took out spies, treacherous piles of leaves and that stack of trash that was hiding a spy or a rabid squirrel.

And people now worry about burning their hands on the EZ Bake Oven.

Most of our favorite toys were not unlike Barkley's here. They were inexpensive, simple and fueled by imagination, not batteries or computer components.

As children, we'd wait patiently with the dog for that first break in the weather, that first slice of spring sun bursting from the sky, opening cold fissures in the landscape. Snow had been fun, but we were tired of the very bitter cold in the last days of winter; stampeding flurries that swirled around the family home with all of the order and elegance of a hockey game, keeping even the hardiest kid indoors.

Summers were anticipated glory. We'd be out after breakfast and play all day, with kids gathered up from around the area, a posse of potential. We'd drink from the hose if we got thirsty and ripped more than one pair of knees out of a pair of jeans, which our mothers would patch, not replace. We offered up skinned knees as homage to the ancient gods of play, exposed our faces to the sun, gaining confidence in our movements, in ourselves, breathing deeply, nourishing ourselves on the scent of grass and the occasional peanut butter and jelly sandwich.

Our play burst out of something within our own minds, shouting forth as we charged the next hill with a bag of plastic soldiers in tow, darting past "throwing grenade guy" with "bazooka guy" to take a spot of land. To us, with the agile minds of children, it was all real. We scurried between small valleys and miniature cliffs. An empty Styrofoam cup with the end cut out with our pocketknife became a tunnel; a scoop of dirt became a foxhole. Overhead was a peaceful bowl of summer sky, below, the happy shouts of children calling forth from smoky battlefield fires that only we could see. The sound of the barrage was both remote and near, our childlike voices providing the sound effects, a vibration in the earth sensed with our minds, rather than felt, as our battalions moved onward, taking more ground.

We advanced until we reached the neighbor's yard, a pristine landscape where the war had not reached, where there would be no quarter given, where soldiers were not to pass and disobedience would be death. Mess with the neighbor's flowerbed, and the troops would be put to rest, the commanding forces grounded. No cookies either, the ultimate punishment.

Such were the days of my childhood. We were immortal; the clouds rushing by faster than our troops could advance. Glorious days. Only darkness or the sound of the dinner bell would bring us in, dirty and hungry and aching to be outside again, and then curled up in sleep with our dog there beside us.

So I understood Barkley and his quest for the perfect toy. But I would have to make sure he got one that would not harm him.

The hard rubber toys in which you could place a treat seemed like a good find. But though Dad's dog loved hers, Barkley wasn't all that interested in his, unless you inserted an entire steak in the middle. His favorite toys were the yellow tennis ball and sturdy fabric covered bones and balls, especially the one with a cord on it that you could wind up and throw.

Still, I missed the look of pure excitement on his face when he heard the first "SQUEEEEK!" of a toy.

A friend of mine had just opened a store that had both a bakery of pet treats and pet gifts and one of the product lines were these "indestructible" dog toys. They were a thick material, heavily corded with thick stitching, allegedly resistant to even the toughest of teeth, guaranteed. Made with bright colors and shaped like an assortment of small animals, they were tempting. They were also pretty expensive. But I got him the biggest and toughest one, Larry the Lobster and presented it to him, thinking that I had purses that cost less than that.

Larry lasted much longer than other toys. Approximately

fifteen minutes longer. I removed the remains in the bucket and took it back to the store, as it did say "guaranteed."

The girl working that day was not my friend, but a new employee. She looked at my receipt and the remains and said "you don't get a refund if you put it through a wood chipper."

"I didn't," I said. "My black lab did this" and showed her a picture of the carnage. She looked doubtful, so I waited to show it to my friend later, who got a good laugh out of it.

I got my refund, and the quest for the indestructible squeaky toy would resume.

12

Penned Up

There are things that are as simple and perfect in their execution as they are in their planning. Tasks that, in retrospect, you can hold up for inspection as if they were a piece of blown glass, clear, perfect and pristine in form, perfectly shaped, without flaw.

This dog pen was not one of them.

Barkley was long past having "accidents" in the house but for the occasional "I ate too fast. . . urp!" barfing. But he was enough of a "what's this, let me chew on it and see!" when he wanted attention that I needed a place he could safely hang out, rather than run loose while I cleaned or rearranged furniture.

But I did not want him to run loose in the basement either as I had some household items stored there, that could be mistaken for a chew toy. "Gee Mom, I know it looked like a lamp shade to you, but I swear, I saw one of these at the pet mart."

I'd gotten the water cleaned up from the flooding down here

after the massive rains and a bigger, better sump pump put in. The front yard landscaping was also upgraded to help keep water away from the house. There should not be any further flooding issues and I was confident Barkley would be content down here for short periods of time.

So I got some wood, some chicken wire, and some cement blocks, attempting to build a large "run" in the basement. There he could run and play safely where it was dry and comfortable in temperature.

The chicken wire was being, shall we say, recalcitrant, and I wished I had some help. But I needed to get this done. I had a work assignment that was going to take me out of town for several weeks, and I did not want the live-in dog sitter to worry about Barkley eating her stuff during the day. With my flight the next day, I was hoping I'd not have to ask for help. As adults, sometimes it's hard to ask for help that is easy to seek as a child.

In my childhood days, there was usually someone helping me in my youthful adventures; and it was in the form of a tall, lanky redhead, otherwise known as Big Bro.

He and I were not all that far apart in age. The difference was enough that the divide that is adulthood came early, but not enough that we were anything but inseparable as children. For unlike many of my friends, who merely tolerated their siblings, we were the best of friends, coming into this home from a shadowed past, one that I do not remember myself, but from which our final displacement from this earth would ever truly dispossess us of.

Our adoptive parents were strict, and we knew that disobedience would merit punishment. Some forms of it, like a declaration of liberty, were worth it. Taking the TV apart when we were in grade school was almost worth it even though we found out that moms will freak out when their children play with large explosive tubes. We won't mention switching the dual controls on Mom and Dad's electric blanket ("I'm hot! Dang it! I'm freezing! Why am I hot! Are you hot?")

Our parents encouraged us to explore and think for ourselves, opening our minds up to everything they could. TV was a treat, not a babysitter. Books were plentiful, and the library was often a stop on a bicycle that had a basket that could carry ten books home. There were no expensive vacations and resorts. There were museums and historic buildings, old trains and mighty dams that spanned rivers full of steelhead trout, creatures always searching, even as they yearned to be home. So with that, we had our hand in many an exercise in the laws of physics versus childhood, such as:

(1) The Mattel Thingmaker should have been named "stupid should burn" even as the stink bugs make great ammo.

(2) The child's wood burning tool does not do a good tattoo on a doll's arm (we'd not as yet grasped Polymers, Thermosetting and Thermoplastic and their resultant

melting points).

(3) Potato guns were designed for real potatoes; Mr. Potato Head is just going to lose his hat and Midge, brave redhead that she was, is going to lose a limb even with G.I. Joe's big bazooka scotch taped to her side. And, finally

(4) The superman cape from Halloween does *not* enable one to fly.

But the limits we stretched were also physical, racing our bikes up and down the block, no helmets or knee pads, as fast as we could make those bikes go. We'd launch an assault up into the embankments of distant foothills, breathing harder and harder, gulping air in and pushing it back out, like some tiny steam engine, until there was no breath left, the last bit escaping the lungs as our hearts surged upward. We went until we could not, salty liquid bursting out from pores and tear ducts, the sweat of freedom that finally stopped us at the summit as we captured up our breath again. Then we'd ride our bikes down the hill again, shouting into the wind and never feeling tired.

Every place was our playground. We played spy and pirate, explorer and soldier; sometimes interchanging the roles as only children can. We were Roger Ramjet on the tail of N.A.S.T.Y. (National Association of Spies, Traitors and Yahoos). We were Napoleon Solo and Illya Kuryakin; we were Lewis and Clark. We crossed undammed ponds, slippery rocks and slippery slopes, the creeks of the woods being our oceans to brave. We shot fake weapons in fake battles, helping our mortally wounded past enemy lines. We would lift them up, scraped knees the only mark of our fallen, keeping them alive even as we knew they were already gone, remembering and forgetting there in that same instant that we could not save them.

There were nights under the stars in the backyard, looking for satellites tracking across the sky. There were lines of gossamer spider web cast from a cherry rod out into the lake, as we floated on inner tubes drifting into our teens. On such days we discussed everything from history to funny cars, to how I hoped we'd never die old and unwanted in the nursing home where I volunteered after school. What could be worse than ending our days in a small room, surrendering to that tiled space, all of our wants and needs and even independence? What could be more fearful than lying in bed alone as from the hallways come no visitors, but only a dulled, rattling saber of loneliness and distress? No, that would not be for us; rather we would go out in a quick burst of honor, the brief fatal blaze of a fine blade, setting us free from our pain and suffering.

As I worked down in my basement, getting the ramparts of Barkley's confinement put into place, I dreaded having to leave him with someone else to care for him here, for the better part of a month, on a job assignment far away. I realized how much he'd grown; almost adult sized, but for a thin shadow that is the form of his recent youth.

Big Bro and I weren't much different, growing up tall and lean, and oh, too quickly. There was the discovery of cars, of the opposite sex, of the wonderful merits of coffee, mornings sitting with brew too hot to drink or even to hold in our hand, claiming that implicit, infinite quality of heat impervious even to its own dissipation, as were we, there on the edge of adulthood.

Then, before you know it, he was gone, off to the Navy, to the adventures we both yearned to experience. I never wanted to be the one left behind, but I was. As he drove away in the blue panel van, in which echoed the sound of so much laughter as we learned to drive, learned our limits, and the speed at which one could lose everything, the tears came as only undammed water can flow.

Now so many years later, our lives curved back into themselves, caught up in the obligations and outcomes that adulthood brings and, whether consciously or not, in the words and affairs of the world that are as undeniable as they are inescapable. The antics of children had seemed so small in the light of my life now, but in looking at the growing form of this dog, I realize they are not. For in those memories, of discovery, of risk, of devotion, we set a fixed distance between the boundaries of the outside world and ourselves. We hold ourselves, if only for this moment, separate from time.

Barkley picked up my hammer in his mouth and started running around the basement with it, pleased with his new toy, even as he struggled to hold its weight. I thought of the past, of bikes and trails and the sound that a piping hot stink bug makes when you hit your target right between the shoulder blades.

I am going to miss Barkley very much when I'm gone, but tonight, I think I'll call Big Bro. He and I have not talked much lately, with careers that fill our time. But I will call him tonight. Across a thousand miles, I will not ask for his help, only his prayers, as I set out on a solitary journey that's getting harder and harder to make, now that I have a little four-legged one waiting for me.

13

"Rollin', Rollin', Rollin'..."

Moving truck information lay around me on the table. I was transferring to another job location, in another state, as our workplace downsized and my particular position was being eliminated. I could stay at the small physical location I was in, in a different job. Or I could transfer to another, bigger office where I could continue the same work, and have better promotion potential.

I had been thinking that buying such a big house had not been the best of ideas. The housing market in our town had tanked badly, the biggest employer in town shutting down. Keeping this house as a rental was not a good idea. It was too big for the average renter, and if the market continued downward, I'd soon be underwater, even with an $80,000 down payment. It was time to cut my losses and look ahead to what I hoped would simply be a new adventure: Barkley.

Fortunately, there were several opening, in varying parts of the country. I accepted the one that would keep me in the Midwest, which I loved and in which I had made friends.

Leaving the house would be tough, the walls I'd textured and painted myself, the pictures of happier times with family, pictures of Barkley, jumping up to catch a ball, making me laugh, even on the most stressful of days. But I was finding out the fancy subdivision lifestyle was not for me, everyone seemingly trying to outdo one another in possessions that many could scarce afford. Never into fashion, I had Yoda pants but no Yoga pants, which all the women seemed to wear, and the first time I dropped the "bodily fluid clean up kit" on the ground out at the collective mailbox, I realized I'd likely not be asked to a block party.

Before I moved though, I knew I should go visit my Dad out on the West Coast, to explain the change, making sure he understood that career-wise, it's possibly a good thing, for myself, as well as him. My Stepmom whom he married after Mom died, a wonderful lady herself, was recently diagnosed with cancer that had gone to the lymph nodes and he had made mention of maybe living with me if she passed soon. This house then, would not work, the bedrooms and full baths, all upstairs, stairs he could no longer navigate—having trouble with them a year ago, on his last visit.

I'd hate to see him leave his home, our childhood home, with so many memories there. Walking into the house, I could see the marks of our lives there, framed pictures on the walls, things we crafted for our parents when we were kids. There is the ceramic squirrel I made in grade school with a teacher overseeing the firing. It is a small statue that looks more like zombie than squirrel yet still to this day it sits on Dad's desk. There is a tiny pitcher Big Bro made. Then there are other things, other memories, one of Dad's many hats perched next to a pair of boots, curtains my mom had sewn, their shadows lingering on the wall where the family found comfort and acceptance around the family dinner table.

When our small family gathers, we share the memories without even speaking of them, as they are woven into the fabric of our lives. Those things we loved as children remain fixed forever in our memory, and will, until we cease to breathe. Wherever we are, wherever we live, our fondest memories haunt those places where we remember comfort given, the sound of laughter, those places that contain our happiest moments.

I wander around my house today, cataloging what needs to be sold or given to charity as I downsize and stage the house for sale. I see an old photo album. It was one that was at my family's home, one of Mom and Dad's youthful days, which Mom had handed me before she died.

Children tend to think of their parents as always having been old, of not experiencing life, its heartaches and its joys. Certainly I was no exception to that thinking growing up, at least until I found the photos. There was a framed photo of them there at home when they were first married: my parents seated on a prim and proper chair that looks about as comfortable as an old Lutheran church pew. Dad's hand was resting on her folded hands, not as an expression of ownership, but as confirmation of the love that shone from his eyes. There was a photo of their Silver anniversary, Mom looking tired but still beautiful. But the album of their youth was something I had never seen before that day.

In it were pictures of Dad's family, some of whom I had never seen. One was that of my grandfather, looking enough like my uncles that I knew instinctively who he was. Dad never once spoke to me of his dad, who died long before I came along. Mom said not to ask about him, alluding to things we knew enough, even young, not to ask further about. It's hard for me to imagine my loving, laughing dad, coming from a background that was anything but happy. It was as if he was miscast for a time and knowingly accepted that role for reasons worth his enduring it, but not of sharing it.

Mom simply said that he, his siblings and mother, were dealt a harsh reality in that home and to leave it at that. Dad still has a picture of his mom on his dresser, a woman whose eyes had seen so much, a look I later recognized, yet she still looked proudly into the camera. Her jaw was set, her mouth a thin, tired line, features forged in the heat of soul or environment, eyes alive and determined in a face of fired clay. He did not mention her often, but the picture of her was carefully framed and dusted, where he could see it as he got up before dawn to dress and go to work to care for his family.

A picture, but few words. But decades after she was gone, unknowingly driving him past the place where she was accidentally struck and killed by a car while walking, he broke down and cried. It was a sound I never expected to hear from him, an echo of heartbreak that sounded from that trammeling memory, never to be mentioned again.

As I box things up, I come across that old photo album. I remember it as being in one of the deep drawers at home, something Mom gave me to preserve and protect when she was gone. I peeked into it at the time and saw small squares and scraps of time, and a whole bunch of young people I did not know. I looked at it for a bit, but then, with the casual disinterest that is youth, I put it away. Now here it is, perhaps I'd best look through it, to see if it is something Dad would want to have back.

Barkley grabbed a kitchen towel off the counter like it was a baton in a race, and went shooting up the stairs, probably to see if he could find a pair of underwear to go with it. The photo album would have to wait.

14

Scraps of Time

Most of my things were packed up and in the moving truck. A few things were going into the car to make the drive to the new home in another state, things I would not want to get lost. In addition to Mom's cookbooks, there were a few pictures for the mantle, some fragile dishware and some photo albums, one of which is the album I stumbled across the other day. As Barkley snoozed, uneasily, not understanding what was happening, I thumbed through it. Barkley was not the only one uneasy. Was I up to the task of caring for Dad in his impending grief and declining health, if that was what he wished? As a child, I might have prayed about it, but as I went into adulthood, I seemed to have fallen away from that, recognizing God, just not particularly familiar with him anymore, like a childhood friend one remembers fondly, but doesn't look up when in town.

I opened up the book. There was a lifetime in those photos, all of the people in them, except Dad, long gone. The photos lay there on my table now, echoes of laughter and human touch--spent shades of eternal desires within mortal hearts, captured in a moment of time. How many times have I been in his house and not closely looked at them?

We miss so much as we rush through life, here or there. We race as if headed south before that first icy blast of winter, race with silent feathering of rigid wing, so driven in that instinctual quest for something, that we miss the perfect sanctuary standing in stark relief against the failing sky. We fly to work, to home, to heartache, with hurried pace, and as if we functioned in a steadfast conviction that time were an illusion.

In our flight, we often soar blindly, missing cues, missing direction.

There is another photo, but one I only carry in my head. It is of a ruined house that stood near a tiny little farmhouse in the Southern plains, where I lived when I was a young bride. The newer home was likely built right next to it; the owners either too broke or weary to tear the original down. You see homes like that, rising gaunt against overgrown thickets, abandoned, left to sky and soil.

I noticed it because of the trees planted between my house and its remains, the branches now growing through openings in the roof of the original homestead, time and decay dissolving its structure. I softly approached it one day. I was alone, placing my steps carefully among the footprints of invisible deer, which left their mark on beds of slain flowers. As I entered what was once the main living area, I was careful not to fall through rotten floors, just to take a look at something I'd lived near and never noticed.

From the trees, I noticed the fledgling leaves lying as hands against the roof of the house, the branches jutting into splintered form, rain coming inside, streaming flatly upon the driving air, moving in. Squatter's rights. Ruin, mold, rot was evident in everything, yet something caught my eye, a glint. It was a doorknob made of glass, sparkling even under the layer of dirt that had settled on everything. Probably a wedding gift for a bride from back East, who had come to this house in the 1800s when it was built.

I took it, and cleaned it off and set it where it could be admired. How long did it lie there, disregarded upon its possession? A hundred years? I'll never know. It is simply one of those little things, important things, owned but not cherished, allowed to gather dust and never truly seen.

It was on my last visit to Dad's to inform him of the move and the house I intended to purchase for us, when I thought of this again. I was out behind his house, clearing out some downed limbs. My eyes were constantly on the move, watching for places I may stumble and fall. How well though, do I see the world, in what is so familiar to me? A thunderstorm stirred overhead, one rather late for this time of year, when snow was spotting the mountains. The air smelled of a burnt match, my form creating unpalatable shadows against a stand of trees. Up ahead there was a flash of light, a rumble of thunder, the sound not racing away in a flash of its own, but ringing in my ears, as if the sound had congealed in the air, waiting to be found.

I'd best hurry to the house, the storm was getting close. As

I ran, I saw it, behind the old apple tree. It was a crumbling crudely made grave marker, tiny, as if for a small thing, a piece of wood washed clean of words but not thoughts. A memory came to me in a flash of light. It was of a small bird I had found fallen from a nest, injured. I had attempted to save it, the wind whipping its small chirp up and away like a tiny, fragile scrap of cloth against the wind, where only the sky and a small child could view it. My Mom knew well it was futile, but let me try, feeding it with a dropper and keeping it warm. It was to no avail, and Mom tenderly wrapped up its taut, silent form and laid it in the ground. She gently laid it away, back behind the house, where we had a small funeral service. I cried as only the innocent can.

How had I forgotten, I thought? I stood there looking, as several raindrops spattered against my face, holding me as sheets of lightning lit up the sky, the clouds swollen as if with child, waiting to release life. In my mind, I was still back there at that small moment of my childhood, memories released. In my mind I was not hurrying as an adult, I was running as a child, with the hurried stroke of a piston engine--wet, skinny, tireless, waiting only to get into the house and see Mom for a hug and warm comfort.

But decades later, I am in my own home, one I have just made the decision to leave, a decision not easily made and one which brings with it, already, the regret of losing something. I looked around; really looked around. It was just four walls. But that is not a home, it is what is inside that matters, photos of my life, names within a Bible I need to open again, Grandma's cookbooks and too many dog toys covering the floor, tripping hazards strewn about with love.

We all have our markers of remembrance; we have our memories. I've another picture to add to that family album, one of my grandfather's grave in the mountains of Montana, where Dad made a special trip recently. It was not to a place he had ever been in my growing up, the power that created that place from which he could not wait to escape, had in turn, taken him safely away from it, to a place where he could be happy without forgiving it. It was time to go back.

On the gravestone was my grandfather's name, the dates of his birth and early death, and the etched images of saddled horses, standing as if waiting for someone to mount up and ride away. With Dad's age and health, the trip was not an easy one to visit that grave and make, as he said, his peace with his Father of earth and of Heaven.

That picture joins the many others on my mantle, being packed up, all weaving together to form a history, a family. My family, the one that needs me now. It is all there in those small squares of paper, small signs of love, given and maintained. It is felt in the small strokes from a hand on a tired brow, and heard in the small strokes of fingers upon slain wood, strumming out inarticulate measures, praying they are heard.

It is a tree that grows close to home, its branches breathing against the house upon the infinite air, driving in an open window the forlorn scent of its need. It is the glow of a fire, the subtle wag of a tail. It is things that are felt, not seen, small things that bring joy, when we learn to let go of the past, of love that has always been around you and will forever remain, simply waiting for the light that would make you see.

Barkley nudges my hand, pointing me toward the door.

15

Moving Days

The car was packed, and the moving truck was already on its way. I'd been selected for a position in a Midwest city, one with the potential for promotion over time. The house here was selling, at a huge loss given the market, but at least it had a buyer.

Things are changing; my Stepmom's diagnosis of cancer, Dad's talk of moving in with me after she's gone, something he swore he'd never do. I found a little ranch house in that Midwestern city I am moving to, bigger than I would have bought for myself, but a lot less fancy and still much smaller than this house. It will provide him his own rooms, and bath, with an entrance without steps for him.

This house stands empty. Only a few folks have been inside, a few neighbors, my parents, a couple of friends and a few dates, none of whom seemed to like dogs, which was becoming more important. We're better off moving on, even alone, I tell Barkley, there's a big world out there with lots of things to do and people to meet.

He's only three years old. I wonder if he will miss this place,

Barkley and I made one last trek around the neighborhood and the woods behind before we left for the first leg of our journey. The moving truck had another stop to make so we would have time to travel and catch up. So many trips we'd made around these blocks. Barkley sniffed everything, pointing to the occasional piece of trash or blowing leaf, as I steered him toward the common area to do his business, rather than on someone's lawn. He, of course, would only lift his leg, and then continue on, for Barkley was always looking for something, a bright picture window, a family seated in front of it at the dining room, enjoying dinner. He'd then dash over to their lawn and squat to do the rest of his business, all right in front of their dinner. Kids squealed and giggled, adults shot me looks that were daggers, as I would wave an apology. Then, I'd go clean up the pile, scolding him yet again, as we walked off, my cheeks blazing with embarrassment, his head held up proudly with a "that was the biggest one yet!"

We took one last walk out into the openly wooded area that runs for a half mile behind this new development, back to a little pond where he first learned to swim. Tonight, I stood at the crest of the rise of sand and dirt that made up the lip of this water filled bowl. Man made or nature made; it was hard to tell, for the perfect shape of the pond. But given the location, it was probably man made. The moon cleaved the pale waste that was sky, the sun having left like low tide, leaving this place in the shadow, just the form of a red haired woman and the dark grieving of earth.

I looked down and saw it, the pale abandoned nest of a Canadian goose; the goslings long having been hatched if the eggs survived both rising waters and predators. I pictured the water moving, like slow waves, but it was as still as I. We both seemingly waited for something, an act of fate, of destiny, the irrevocable sentence of time that's passed or perhaps, an invitation.

I wondered if I came back in ten years, if this place would still be here. Or would it be plowed into yet another row of Monopoly houses, another neighborhood of lives and love, fights and frustration and unborn children who can't wait to grow up so they can leave this place, then wish desperately that they could return.

They say you cannot go home again, and perhaps as far as a childhood home, that is true. But what of the memories of other places we hold firm in our mind's eye? Some of them we have a name for, our elementary school, the river where we dove as far out as we could into the dark water, a place where church bells rang. In the Book of Genesis, the world was formed out of wind and chaos. "And God called the dry land Earth; and the gathering together of the waters called he Seas." Sometimes, the incredibly complex can be summed up in one word. Some things have no words at all, their form remembered only in the etchings of tears.

But of those places, both named and unnamed, there are places you are drawn back to, years later, praying they are not changed, and knowing it will not be so.

I hope in ten years Barkley and I can come back here, if only to wave at the house in which I raised him to adulthood, as to an old friend.

16

"Calgon, Take Me Away"

Many of you remember those old Calgon commercials with the beautiful but frazzled woman leaving crying kids, barking dogs and chores behind for a soak in a giant bathtub full of bubbles.

Although there are some things that even a bath won't fix, having one is a nightly ritual for me. In the morning, I get a super quick shower, just to wash my hair and go. Nights though are my time to relax. The new, smaller house had a pretty small bathroom but it did have a big 1960s style tub, narrow with tall sides, which I could fill up deeply with water.

I used to enjoy that evening bath as part of a road trip, but it seems that lately, the tubs have gotten smaller, and more and more hotels, even nicer ones, just have a huge, built-for-two shower, but no actual bathtub. I miss the big tubs while traveling. There was a hotel in Ireland that had the narrowest bathtub I'd ever been in, that was also the deepest. After a red eye flight, I filled it up, crawled in and promptly fell asleep. Outside, the snow tumbled like a crashing plane, only to land on my windowsill in soft silence, but for the sound of traffic, much of it, like me, strangers looking for something familiar.

There have been so many strange places in which I've laid my head over the years, so many miles. The wheels have clicked past places of opulent wealth and desolation more profound than ruin, velvet sunsets of plush richness and the cold iron dawn marked by bullets and a soldier's iron footprint. They've clicked past solitary countryside and crowded highways dotted with one too many crashes, which slow everything down to a crawl. Sometimes the first responders are simply standing on the median, with no hurry to tend to that which is past tending. Cars creep past, the morbidly curious, heads up as if listening, a profoundly studious and distracted listening for that which they will never hear, nor were ever intended to hear.

On such trips, by the time you get to the hotel, you can either raid the mini bar or take a long bath. Given that a thimbleful of booze in a mini bar is more expensive than what I had for dinner, I choose a long bath, and many a night was spent with just the cooling water and me, there before sleep.

Still, coming home from work tonight, even after an uneventful day, the bathtub still invited. Barkley, however, saw the bath, not as his person's chance to relax, but competition for my time.

I usually waited until just before bed, when we'd already had some time to play, and had enjoyed food, treats and one last walk, hoping he'd leave me in peace for just thirty minutes.

If I shut him out of the bathroom, he whines like I'm in some dire danger from sources unknown. If I let him in, he tries to:

(1) drink the water *out of* the tub

or

(2) sit and stare at me with a look that's designed for a maximum of guilt.

How do you explain to an animal that what to him is playtime without him is sometimes my only way of unwinding? It's that time when the day drops back to deep thoughts, the ones you were trying to get past, the work that is piling up, that tattered picture hidden in your wallet of someone whose eyes are focused on a place that did not include you. It's respite from that ticking of a clock in the next room that reminds you that time drives on like fiery steel, overtaking even the swift. You can think too much about such things; the face in the mirror, the soul's own inquisitor, or you can ram your small plastic cruise ship into a giant rubber ducky and make explosion sounds.

I opt for the latter.

Over the few years in which Barkley has been part of my household, bath time has become a routine. I keep the water level low enough that he cannot drink out of it. I make sure my bath toy collection is kept out of sight and reach so we can avoid that whole "chase the dog and the last attack class boat around the living room without my clothes" thing. I've learned not to let him make me feel guilty with the looks, still reaching over to pat his head every so often and talking to him of my day.

But tonight, after a busy time of adjusting to a new job, and new home, with lots to be painted or fixed, I just wanted some "alone" time. Barkley and I faced each other like chess pieces, the Queen this time, not going to be taken by a mere Black Knight. He's learned the command "stay out" used in the kitchen when I'm cooking, so I tried it in the bath, to hopefully get him out of the room, yet leaving the door open so he can see I'm OK.

"Out, Barkley! Out!"

It worked! With a sigh, he turned and exited, going out of eyesight into the hall, the sound of his toenails clicking on the tile, and then muted by carpet. He was only about three feet away, but the way the door and tub are aligned, I couldn't see him.

I should have tried this sooner, I thought, as I finally set my head back to relax as the water cooled.

Something flew past my field of vision. I opened my eyes. There, next to the tub, was a rolled up pair of socks. I heard a gentle whine. I ignored it. A minute or two later, here came another rolled up pair of socks (Dad isn't the only one that can roll up socks into the size of a tennis ball).

From the hallways came another gentle whine. I knew that sound as the "I have something of yours, come get me" whine.

He won't harm the object, won't even play with it, unless you look.

Another pair was tossed into the bathroom. I pulled myself out of the water so I could see what is happening.

Barkley was *tossing* the socks into the room with his mouth trying to get my attention. Apparently, my packed and open suitcase was a veritable buffet of socks tonight. I was either going to drag myself out of the tub with that ponderous impetuosity of defeat or I could stay here while, one by one, my undergarments were flung around the room as the evening's entertainment.

I stood up, put the socks on the counter and invited him in to sit by me on the bath mat.

As I crawled back in the tub, I realized I did not put away the tub toys, there floating within view.

SPLOOSH!

I now had an eighty pound lab in the tub with me, Mr. Rubber Duck in his mouth, as happy as could be to have bath time with his person.

I'm beginning to think the designers of all of those tub-less hotel rooms own Labrador retrievers.

17

Do Not Ask for Whom the Dog Barks, He Barks for Thee

We had survived the winter in our new house, the snow here, not nearly as deep as in the last state we lived in, although I shoveled more than I had planned. I loved having a fenced yard though, even a modest chain link one. I could let Barkley in and out without leash, wind or cold. He seemed to know however, when I was not looking my best—at which point he refused to come in from the depths of the yard until I came on the deck in fuzzy bathrobe, wild red hair and slippers to call for him.

"Barkley, if you're trying to help me meet a nice guy, this is *not* the way to do it."

Sometimes I'd have to go out to get him to quit barking at the ducks, at the geese, at a leaf floating by on the surface of the pond. I was trying to teach him *not* to bark at nothing, only at a real threat. I'm not sure if it was helping. Sometimes he'd just stand by the front gate and selectively bark as if he had some form of Doggie Tourettes.

I was trying to teach him good from bad barking habits. So if he barked at a tiny bunny I'd say "Barking BAD!" If he barked at a stranger hanging around the front sidewalk, even if likely harmless, he heard "Barking GOOD!" He then got a little treat. That kept more than one door to door salesman away as his bark sounded like it was coming from a huge Mastiff. He wasted *no* time with the allowable barking, wanting that treat as soon as possible.

He also knew the word "company." You might bark at company, but "company" meant someone was coming over and that meant food and treats and people that might be suckered with big brown eyes into giving him goodies. With that word, he would still bark, and loudly, but his tail would be wagging.

The whole backside of the house had windows that faced the pond that ran between two blocks of homes. Barkley always assumed his position of protector on the little loveseat against the window, looking out across the back of it at his territory as it grew dark, a small form of courage, and a heart big enough to contain the world.

One evening we were relaxing to some quiet music, Barkley in his usual position on the love seat. The lights were dim; the outside lights not on yet. The shrubs formed foreign, almost, ghostly shapes, the limb of the tree a black gash across the moon.

I could hear music from a distance. Across the water, it looked like the neighbors were having some party, windows open, adults in and out, smoke from the grill. It wasn't overly noisy, I was just aware of it.

Then I noticed movement behind my chain link fence. I looked out. It was dark, but in the flash of a cigarette lighter I could see it was the kids of that neighbor and their friends, probably sneaking out of the house during the boring parental entertainment. They likely figured no one would see as they lit an illicit cigarette trying to look both older and cool, achieving neither. They likely weren't up to any mischief, but I didn't want them sitting out against my fence, throwing their cigarette butts onto my property.

Barkley had a low growl in his throat. I looked at him and said "company," as the kids weren't up to any harm, just teens being teens. But I had no intention of this becoming a habit and picking cigarette butts out of my yard every Saturday morning.

I looked at Barkley, his tail now tail wagging, and pointed out toward the fence, and said "Barking Good!"

I then opened the door, the porch light off. But for the light across the pond, it was pitch dark outside, Barkley fading like the intangible form of some dark, quiet shadow into the silent night.

I half expected him to launch into the bark immediately, but he did not.

Instead, he rushed at the fence in the darkness, invisible on the air, until he was six inches behind them, at which point he launched into a full scale bark.

BARK BARK BARK BARK BARK

I heard the squeals and heard the rushing of movement, as the kids *flew* like a flock of pheasants away from those imagined teeth and that fence. I'd be willing to bet at least one of them wet their pants.

I love my dog.

18

The Deep End

It had been quite a day. I'd pulled a particularly late shift, gotten about three hours of sleep, then had to drop off the used four wheel drive extended cab, four-door truck I'd recently bought, at the local dealership. I had the day off and it needed a service check that had already been put off.

It was late fall, and the day dawned grey and chilled, clouds slung low to the ground, appearing not to hold moisture, but rather dust, the sparse ragged edges of it, looking like cloth flung down upon the ground. We were all settled in the new house, and the new job was going well, coworkers warm and welcoming, but I still hadn't made what I would call a "friend" outside the workplace. Still, I'd not lived here all that long and I had Barkley.

There is this little "grump" sound he makes if he's woken early. Normally he rises from the puffy Beignet of a dog bed as soon as my eyes are open, but today, he just curled up and went back to sleep.

OK, Barkley, I'll drop the truck off, then come back and feed you.

I looked like something he'd drug in from the yard, hair in disarray, dark circles under my eyes. But I had to get the vehicle in so I could get some more sleep before picking it up, and perhaps then, enjoy a quiet night off.

I threw on sweats and put the red curls in a scrunchie, not bothering with comb or makeup. I then drove it over and dropped it off, leaving the keys with the service manager and walking a short distance home.

Once home, it was time for food, playtime with Barkley and some serious shut eye.

The alarm went off mid-afternoon. I got a shower and did my hair, putting on makeup and my spiffy leather coat and went to get the truck, feeling on top of the world with six solid hours of sleep on top of the "nap" that was last night.

As I walked in, the same manager greeted me with "it didn't take as long as we expected but wasn't it nice that your mom dropped it off this morning."

My mom?

This day was not turning out the way I planned.

Still, as I drove home, I remembered I had an evening to myself.

After letting Barkley out in the yard briefly to play, I unloaded a few things from my truck, made some tea and sat down. When I passed down the hall, he was sound asleep in the middle of my bed; I was still too tired to make him move, and I simply went out into the family room and sat down.

Now this was more like it. It was getting later, the shadows falling; the night soon to arrive as the day gathered like folds of warm cloth against my legs. It was a beautiful view; as past my chain link fenced yard is the retaining pond of clear water. It's not deep, but it extends the whole length of the block, a scattering of homes on each side. Only one neighbor has a fence, the other neighbor's yard open, giving me a good view of the water. I breathed deep as I watched the trees, a few stubborn leaves attached like weathered flags clinging to an ancient pole, the branches forming a shield from the setting sun, one of a familiar order in this new house. I had the whole evening off. I would get a long bath once it was dark, read for a bit and then get a good night's sleep. Until then, there was nothing to do but go to the kitchen and make more tea, gathering those thoughts that scatter around the room as if the window had been left open.

The doorbell was ringing. It was still light out, and I see the red hair of a little girl from a few doors down through the dining room window. I was guessing it was for a school candle fundraiser or candy sale, and reached for my purse as I opened the door.

"Barkley is swimming in the pond."

I wonder for a moment as to how she knew his name, realizing everyone within a half mile has probably heard me outside shouting "Come here!" or "Not again?!"

I reply, "No, he's not, he's inside sleeping on the bed. That must be another black dog."

"No, it's Barkley, he's swimming!" she says as she points.

I look out. He had somehow gotten out, run to the neighbor with no fence and through their yard to the water, where he was swimming laps back and forth behind our house, like he was at the YMCA or something.

How did he get out?

I looked into the laundry room where I hauled in the stuff from my truck. The door to the garage was open, as was the garage itself.

I thanked the little girl and went to fetch him out of the pond.

He did *not* want to come in, the "it's my own personal swimming pool!" look in his eyes. I sat down on the little bench I put up by the water, but had not used and simply waited. That gave me time to add up the multiple likely subdivision codes we would have been breaking at our old house (they're still upset about my painting the front door Winchester Repeating Arms Red).

I don't scold him though. I remember the lure of the water as a youngster. With cold winters and a blue collar economy, my home town was not conducive to pools but we had the YMCA, starting our lessons there as soon as we could toddle near a body of water. I remember a silly little girl's bathing suit, with flowers and some awful skirt thing, and worst of all, a swimming cap. "Why do I have to wear a bathmat on my head?" I lamented to Mom. It smelled like one, and pulled on my hair as it came off. She said, "They don't want long hair in the pool; only boys don't have to wear one."

My answer to that was a short haircut, a very short haircut. Not short enough for someone to think I was a boy, but short enough that I got to use that cap for a turtle transport system when cleaning out their little plastic bowl and not for the pool.

During the school year, we'd head to the "Y" for the occasional family swim night; in the summers we'd go several times a week, chasing each other and the neighboring kids around like seals until shooed out by the lifeguard. Pressure, movement, force and displacement never failed to hold us there, pushing ourselves through the water with strong, growing bodies, never seeming to get old. It wasn't a pool; it was an ocean, full of pirates and sharks, and one's got my leg! No, it's just Big Bro playing tag with me in the water.

A quick rinse off and I'd be back in shorts and a T-shirt, my curly hair still short, drying in the breeze as we rode home in the back of the neighbor's pickup truck. The air would be warm, and the ride would be too short, those two slow miles, down a long, shady street to our homes.

I wasn't going to begrudge Barkley that experience tonight, with those childhood memories of the pool at the YMCA, or even better, on vacation with a hotel pool. There, we'd sleep to time's beguilement and wake to the merriment of the sun, echoing in the perfect splash of water into the deep end, where we threw ourselves, our reason, and restrictions, into the embrace of the depths, knowing it would always accept us.

Barkley was starting to slow and look up to the house. A neighbor wandered over, the mother of the red-headed girl, introducing herself to ask if I'd like to have coffee sometime.

"Sure," I said, as Barkley came out of the water toward us for some attention, happy to be connected again.

19

On Being a Parent

Barkley and Dad were playing out in the yard as I prepared a little scoop of frozen yogurt for them both. He'll tease me that I spoil this dog like a child, and in some ways I do.

He and my Stepmom were out for a visit at my home. Not in preparation for moving him in, but for just a visit and a joyous celebration. My Stepmom's cancer was now in remission, her outlook positive, despite the removal of part of her jaw, and debilitating treatment. I wasn't sure what I was going to do with this big house, at this point, only happy to know, he could stay in his own, for many more years.

We'd have a lot to talk about, he and I.

There is a philosopher's dictum that the unexamined life is not worth living, but certainly there are parts of it we wish we could forget. I've read stories of people that have had a near-death experience, in which they recounted that on arriving on the "other side" they review their entire life, as if on film, good and bad in a wink of an eye. I have a feeling, that if that is true,

I'm going to be looking up at God, hopefully with Barkley by my side, at more than one spot, exclaiming "Did we do *that*?"

But in looking back now, through those retroactive reels of years, there is much to be gained, lessons learned, often at the hands of our parents. As children, we think of our parents as always having been parents, knowing the ways of dealing with the world wisely and automatically, as if being parents somehow bestows instant wisdom. As children, we look up to and emulate them even if perhaps it's not always warranted. Memory can sometimes do that, clouding the past and even the future with what we wish to believe, rather than what is not tolerable for us to accept. As children, we listen and we watch, more than they realize, both good and bad. From it we form our own selves and make our own errors.

From my parents, I learned many things--skills that can mean either imminent disaster or survival, depending on where the pointy end is placed. I remember putting rounds of .22 ammunition through pop and beer cans there in the quarry with my former LEO mom, the slow, deliberate sound descending upon the thick summer air, like a gavel lay down upon wet silence. I remember the feel of the bullet in my hand, that feather balance between good and evil and all the responsibility that holds. I remember mornings in the kitchen with my grandmother, who lived with us until her death, preparing meat that didn't always come from the grocery store and bread that didn't come from a bright plastic package. We'd be up and working as the sun rose from the earth, like the spoke of a wheel, hubbed at a spot on the planet that no map can display.

Even more clearly, I remember Saturdays as I earned my allowance by keeping the family station wagon meticulously clean. Dad and I would laugh and talk as he worked close by on other chores, the branches of the plum trees stirring with our words, Big Bro running past, getting squirted with the hose, his tall, red haired form, the exclamation point to our laughter. I'd go to bed on such days, tired, smelling faintly of car wax, the dollar I earned for the work lying on the dresser with my toys, carefully pressed flat with my hand.

I also learned the outcome of *not* following parental advice that resulted in several rules that should be posted on any shop wall.

(1) Whether negligent, intentional or inadvertent, pulling the trigger puts a big hole in something

(2) Just because it has fur does not mean it wants to be petted

(3) Nose hair is flammable and

(4) Speed may temporarily outwit it, but gravity always wins

For my parents still allowed us room to make our own mistakes, to achieve on our own merit. They did not clean up our messes, do our homework, or excuse any bad behavior. Neither did they support those activities where children were rewarded for just showing up, not winning; behavior my Dad said only further fosters the self-absorbed entitlement that is a parent's personal burden and their offspring's future failure. When we lost at something, we knew we lost, failure being neither sugar-coated nor rewarded. With the loss, came the determination not to lose again. When we won, they were proud because we did it without help.

Not everything we did warranted recognition, as we learned that a shoddy effort has no reward. We tried; we sometimes failed. We suffered the spherical bombing that was dodge ball, we broke the occasional arm. We fell out of that tree limb without a helmet and made things in art class that only a parent would love. We didn't have a lot of expensive toys or gadgets. What we had was even better. The neighborhood was our world to conquer. The grass was our battlefield. In imaginary battle, we howled; arms raised in triumph over outlaws and enemy soldiers. Our lives were not yet dampened by that frantic, immobile urgency that is the awareness of time.

And so we grew up, slightly nicked and dented, but with lessons that kept us alive more than once. I look at a set of pilots wings there on the mantle, and understand that I lived long enough to place them there by realizing that they are only wings, not a special pass from Mother Nature and bad judgment.

For my parents' lessons, I am grateful, just as I am grateful they were both around long enough for me to get to know them as individuals, not just as my parents. I was grateful for a Stepmom who also loved and forgave, and realized that her new home would always be our late mom's home in our hearts, a designation that she was neither jealous of nor worried about.

Several items of Mom's from that home, now reside in my own. There in a drawer, Mom's badge from the Sheriff's Department, Dad's paperwork for his trip to another land where war raged, a trip from which many did not return, dying too young to remember really living. I keep such things as a reminder, not of their time together, but of all the time that they had. For although they were "Mom and Dad," they were also two unique souls, lives joined in one brief shining glimpse out of all time, the remarkable achievement of their union, not their home, not their careers or even their children, but the light they left for us to follow.

Now Dad is here, throwing the ball for Barkley in the backyard, feeding him bits of burger he should not, giving me directions in the car to places I've driven to a hundred times safely, spilling a soda on the couch as he wrestles with a big black lab, both knowing better.

Somewhere the roles have changed, and I'm now the one watching over him. But I do so with a different outlook on it than I expected.

In looking back, I realize that, for them, being a parent was something they learned by trial and error; that mistakes were made and forgiven, even as my own were. They were two imperfect and flawed human beings whose actions were recognition and protection of that brave bargain that is parenthood. For that, I will always be grateful. For that, they will always have my respect, even as they leave me.

So I will be patient with them, just as I learned patience with a black furry dog, who doesn't always mind me, but always loves me. Like Barkley, Dad will always be there for me, the role of protector—one he will not give up, even if he sometimes fails to heed my words, just as I sometimes failed to heed his, either beneath or beyond the knowledge that he had conveyed.

In the room I had fixed up to be his bedroom, there is a plaque on the wall. It's made of wood, a living thing that never slept, never dreamed of the soft perch of birds or the sharp blade of the ax, never mourned the tender leaves that it nourished and abandoned. It's a piece of wood, that which can be warmth, support and shelter, or simply left to lie, forgotten. On it is a picture of praying hands, on a piece of paper, carefully affixed to the wood, the edges carefully singed with a wood burning tool held in small hands. It's crude by most standards, but I remember the pride as a child as I presented it to him with an "I made this!"

It hangs on the wall, still and forever, made without the help of my Father's hands but with all of his love.

20

Where Did the Bacon Go?

The house seemed so empty after Dad and my Stepmom had gone back home. I knew another visit here would be unlikely, the long trip tiring for both of them. I would continue my trips out there on my vacation days.

I usually have a friend that will stay with him as I travel, but a couple of times Barkley stayed overnight at the Doggie Day Camp he enjoys when I have a long day planned. The first time he went there for the day; he came home so excited, with a little report card they gave him. Let's just say, he didn't get straight A's. I'd like to think Barkley was a model child, but I think he was more like one of those teens that ditches class to hang out in the parking lot smoking a cigarette.

I asked if there were problems. They smiled and said it was just the normal ones for new dogs, hogging the toys, spilling his food dish. But he socialized well and was welcome back. Soon, he was used to the routine and got a much better report card, though I still have a photo of him running around with the bucket that held all of the toys in his mouth.

He even found the perfect squeaky toy there, a hard rubber ball with feet and a built in squeaker that he was unable to destroy, one I was able to find on-line. We called it simply "Mr. Squeaky" and although there were days that Mr. Squeaky had to be taken away before Mom got into the Scotch, he loved that toy.

Even with Mr. Squeaky here to play with, he moped a bit after the folks said goodbye. He missed the man that fed him all the treats he wasn't supposed to get, having the decency to at least look chagrined when he threw up after too many little pieces of Dad's cheeseburger. He missed the tiny and kind woman that, though recently more and more forgetful, always remembered his name.

He was back on dry food and wholesome dog treats; vacation was over for both of us.

But there would be company coming in a couple of months, friends from back East to stay for a couple of nights.

The time flew by and soon it was that time. Snacks and drinks were chilling for their arrival, as I would be home late from work.

It was one of those flawless winter evenings, the sky crisp and heavy with thought. Coming back from work, I did not rush, happy that Barkley would have someone he knew there who would keep him company until I got home.

The day I had just left was not a good one and knew I would be carrying the sights and smells of it with me on the drive, perhaps hanging those thoughts of them up somewhere late tonight so I could get some sleep. It was time to think of other, happier things; time to come home and give my dog a hug.

He's the keeper of the sofa, guardian of the throw rugs, and something I never planned on getting, but I did, suckered in by the litter of black fur. The first night home, he slept on my chest as I lay on the couch next to his prepared little kennel of which he wanted no part. I felt the gentle thump against my chest, for he began to give me his heart that very first night, and he, as well, had mine.

Then the days became weeks, and then months, and before you knew it he was my protector, not the other way around. On those days, when the reality of another sanguinary day on this planet took hold, I could escape into the loving affection of a simple game of fetch or a nap for two on the family room couch. That safe spot buffered me, hid me, and helped me distance myself from anything that troubled me, while he and I both left the past in bounding leaps of faith and joy.

He was sound asleep when I got home, giving a soft woof as the back door opened. I gave him a biscuit, and then he promptly went back to sleep outside the guest room door, making sure they did not get up in the middle of the night to eat the last of the treats or something.

In the morning, the sun was out, the memories of the previous day, brushed off of me with the blanket. I was ready to start a new day of fun and laughter. And bacon, I smell bacon.

Someone was cooking breakfast.

I put on my robe and wandered out. Standing in the kitchen was my friend T., with Barkley stationed at his feet. SNAP! Barkley jumped up and grabbed a piece of cooled bacon T. had tossed off of a paper towel to him.

Half of the bacon from the new package was missing.

There were no pieces left on the towel.

"Uh, how many have you given him?"

T. replied, "Oh, five or six. Man he *loves* this stuff!"

"Uh Oh."

"Barkley, backyard, now, out out out," and I herded him out the door, as my friend simply looked on puzzled.

Up it came, bacon, grease, and whatever food he'd already eaten.

At least it wasn't on my carpeting.

Barkley went back inside, and immediately sat at T's feet as he continued to fry more bacon, ready to start it all over again.

21

Stormy Weather

Our first three years in this little ranch house had passed quickly. I loved my job, and even had a promotion, one that allowed for less travel and more time at home with Barkley, which was even better. But this house was much more than I wanted to keep up, with just one person living in it. Dad was firm in his decision that he wanted to stay in his house, even now that my Stepmom was diagnosed with Alzheimer's and he was caring for her himself, at home. I understood. He wasn't lonely even if some days she did not know who he was.

Right now, I could sell this place for what I paid for it, and there had been some interest. The market here was reasonably stable, but not likely to stay that way with one of the biggest employers in the city rumored to be planning another layoff and a new road from the city through here that was bringing more crime. I bought this with the intent of Dad living with me, not just for myself. I could afford it, if I watched my budget. I just didn't want so much space and yard to take care of. I wanted something small and tidy, with a basement or shop to work on projects without having to stand out in a cold garage.

My family still asked if I'd move back West, wondering why I liked living in the Midwest so much, even if the grandparents on my Dad's side were from this state. "There are tornadoes!" they'd say, as if earthquakes, tsunamis, mudslides and sharks that eat surfers like popcorn are just run of the mill worries.

But Barkley and I had made so many new friends here, from the very first day I came back from the local LEO pistol range, with: "Guess what's next to the range Barkley . . . a dog park!" Soon we were getting out more, meeting folks that frequented both places, meeting other dog lovers who were also science and book lovers. One of my online female friends had moved to the local area as well. Soon, I had a small group of friends that would gather in a restaurant or gather in my kitchen, sharing food and stories. I also started going back to church again, after a couple stumbling mistakes with situations and people that only caused hurt. Those were events that made me realize that what I was seeking in life would be best found in the form of my life's beginnings, and that included God as more than a witness to my life, but part of it.

So I had many friends, those that played with me and those that prayed with me. It seems there was always someone around, Barkley's extended family; even if at night it was just Barkley and me. Today was no different, as I turned from the kitchen to spy Barkley on the couch between two people, sitting up with his mouth open as if saying "And there I was, the great Cape buffalo charging at me..." entrancing everyone with his many adventures as we shared some dessert after an outing together.

But there was a forecast for bad weather tonight, with a possibility of tornadoes, so folks headed home before it got dark. I've always loved an impending storm, which is probably why, when I see one on the radar that's forming, I'll be on the porch or outside so I can see the storm approach. There's such strength when air masses collide. Even as a child, I wanted to put my hands up to the illuminated sky and to see if somehow I could hold that power in my small hands. There's just something about it, feeling the change in the temperature and the pressure, the first claps of thunder, the smell of rain.

I've never intentionally chased a tornado, but I understand the fascination, being filled with fear, yet drawn along its deadly path, its very presence a summons to all my foolish blood. I've stood on the porch much too long for safety, as lightning cleaved the sky as a machete, the smell of cordite in the air lingering like gunpowder. I've stood in a hangar door, as thunder echoed like a brace of artillery booming under a gunmetal sky, the power of the sky a transcendent weapon that can form or scar, however we view it, the landscape of our world.

I've learned the hard way that in just a moment things can change, what was once invincible, reduced to ragged form and splintered dreams, what was once strong, lying broken, shadowy and dim beneath a disinterested sky. I've also learned that somewhere within me is the courage to pick up that which remains.

When my friends waved goodbye and headed out, I could see the changes in the sky. It was almost seventy degrees, not as a memory of summer, but as a warning. Warmth, moisture and a November sky usually do not bode well, though it had yet to assume that grey green otherworldly color that has had me load up a transport plane and head in the opposite direction as quickly as possible, more than once in my life. Though the sky brooded low over me, the radio said that the worst of it was still a ways out.

As I came inside, the phone rang, but it was not duty, it was my Dad, watching the weather channel and concerned. No matter how old I get, he worries, age only diminishing his sense of geography which means I get calls if there is a storm in New York or Georgia or Kansas. Indiana, in his mind, is not my residence or the birthplace of his mother, but simply that state in which the meteorologist is always pointing the finger of doom. Sometimes the call wakes me, as the three hour time difference also eludes him on some days. I answer with that forced bravery that at one time he could see through, but can no longer, his mind, though often sharp, sometimes circling in orbit around itself, calling me by the name of someone long dead, yet somehow knowing who I am.

But I did not fuss, for I know that too soon, these calls will cease, a change for which I'm not yet ready. The phone silent again, in the distance comes a train, the sound of wheels on tracks reiterating the syllables of that name, that one small sign of a mind's slow dimming, The rhythm of the train passes into silence, as hard as I try to hear.

I made light of the danger, but looking at the radar, I was a bit concerned as some rotational potential was there. I emailed a friend who lives up in northern Illinois, to see if they were seeing any of it yet. My friend EJ said it was headed more south, right for me. Great.

I watched the radar as the cells approach; letting Barkley out to potty and to come back in before they arrived. As he shook his fur, the rain starting up, the TV was saying "seek shelter." Now, as I continued to watch, I viewed the formation and shape of the cell as a scientist, not as its prey.

When the sirens went off, Barkley and I headed for a bathroom in the interior of the house, with an emergency biscuit, and some big cushions from the couch to pack around us. Barkley showed absolutely no concern for the dangers, trying to hump the cushions as I piled them up. I did not know whether to laugh or cry, even as he eluded my attempts to save him.

I could hear the little TV on the dresser in the next room. The cell with rotation was going north of my town, as they often do, and we emerged from the bathroom, to look out the window to see if any limbs or lines were down. By midnight, the worst of the storms had passed, missing my little town as they always seemed to, splitting north and south of the freeway, leaving in their wake somewhere, a landscape burned with anguish and anger. I had all the lights off while Barkley settled onto his bed, listening as the wind impinged upon the trees, needles of rain piercing the sodden flowerbeds. Outside, the street lamps glowed as if underwater, the air weighted with passing rain as we both fell into sleep.

In the morning I turned on the TV to see about damage, to see the news of a whole town ravaged, not far away, and the images came to me unbidden.

Not so many miles away, the rough skin of the earth lay in ruins, as people climbed from the wreckage to see exactly what they had been left, voices rising as the wind diminished, the infinite voices of human fear and anguish of which we all remember. The first responders arrived, eyes quite wide and filled with something beyond curiosity or horror. They would do their work, lifting up a small still form, draped with the dignity of cloth, lifting it easily as if it had no weight, yet with the movements that showed that underneath that cloth, was borne the iron weight of all of earth and grief. But they continued their task, for between hope and nothing, they would choose hope.

I turned off the news, the pictures still reflected in my eyes. It's easy to ask where God was on such days as houses fell, as disasters rained down, fire in the sky. But I do not ask that perfect bitter prayer, one that has already been uttered.

I thought of the last picture before the screen went dark, a survivor bent down looking for anything of value left from their home. I knew that crouch so very well. I too have assumed that posture, bent down to the ground on bended knee, not weighted down by grief, but balanced rather, in the complete concentration of what may just be the smallest scrap of a life lived, looking around as if guarding it. For some things need guarding, not as protection from some four-legged creature, but those two-legged creatures that move on among both the protected and the protectors, those that will take what is precious even from the fallen.

I was thankful to be safely under a roof, where I could sit in the quiet with my thoughts, as the wind wrapped itself around the building like a thick dark cloth, a glass of amber liquid in my hand that tasted of mist and peat, deep love and grief. As the storms rumbled on eastward my soul was still, thinking of the rumbles of change that were occurring in my life. Some I can control, and some I cannot, those things of life and wind and death that even our beloved God writes upon our hearts at birth. Some of these changes can scar our landscape, as we have seen this night. But some can bring with them a clearing rain, one that lets you see so much more clearly the blessings around you after it has passed.

22

Snow Day

Outside the snow started, the door painting a path out into the white, only one lone dog brave enough to take it tonight. His paw prints left a trail like bread crumbs, delicate and soft, disappearing even as I looked for them with the snow falling down.

The cold and white was going to skirt the edge of my world tonight. I was glad to be in safe and warm, for I remember too many nights out working in the elements as winter shook its fist at the forecast. Tonight, the roads would be mostly empty, nothing else braving the space around us but some poor, cold creatures trying to seek shelter as best they could, a couple of forlorn horses of a distant neighbor, waiting to be brought back into the glow of light in the stable. If I looked out onto the snow, beyond the boundaries of grass and water and horizon, it appeared to come down ever so frantic and furious. A life, these years, can seem to hurry past that way if you let the vision of it trick you, glimpse of white, of black, then gone, when you may least expect it.

This was going to be our last winter in this old ranch style house. I had a party interested in purchasing it in the spring when they moved to this area. I'd lose out on the few thousand I'd put into paint and appliances, and I'd have to tap into savings or borrow to pay the realtor, but it was time to downsize.

It was a decent older home, better than the huge subdivision home I'd given up several years prior, before the transfer, especially with a huge fenced yard which Barkley loved and a view. But the area was building up after that four lane road from the city came through, and what used to be a view of countryside and corn was now mostly subdivisions. Plus, I did not need all of the space, even if the house was modest in construction and price compared to my last home, it was still a lot to maintain as a single woman, one who had barely enough time for a dog, let alone a house.

I enjoyed watching him play in the snow, even as I was happy to do so from the warmth of the house, my reflection in the mirror showing flakes of snow in my hair from opening the door. How did winter get here so quickly? I look in an old mirror, imagining the generations that have looked into that gleaming surface, asking themselves at least once, how did it all fly by so quickly, asking those questions across those years, time they hopefully learned didn't matter, as they savored every last remnant, there in the depths of something they had questioned too long.

Barkley loved the snow. He ran and jumped, tossing the snow up in the air with his nose as I tried to take pictures of him from the porch. The camera failed to capture that movement as he appeared to fly, the steam of his breath, the thudding spray of snow as he landed, laid out in pixeled particles of white. But I wanted to try and capture that moment, between stillness and unbridled motion, where even mass seems to be physically altered, changing from solid muscle to wind the color of night. I look at him and then look at the sky. Both he and I for this moment are becoming "pups" again.

As children, growing up where we did, "snow days" were infrequent. The world did not stop for snow where snow was not uncommon. When we got a snowstorm, we'd be outside the door before the breakfast dishes were even put away. Snow was not cold; it was not work or worrisome. It was a divine benediction which spread itself out onto the world where we waited with glee. Grabbing an inner tube to ride down the cleared foothills, shoving a couple of cookies in ours pockets, we would head out into the dazzling white, heeding the siren call.

There I would simply wait my turn with my tube on the hill called "widow maker," content to just sit and look up into the wonder as we waited our turn. That tube was not my transport to the stars; it was a defiant gesture against the mortality that grew closer to the edge of our vision every year. It wasn't a simple inner tube. It was a defiant shout. It was my shield.

Then I'd launch myself with abandon out into it, flinging my form down onto an inner tube that was traveling downhill much faster than my Dad ever approved. There was nothing but movement and emotion, snow in the amber fire of my hair, my cheeks flushed, body arching up into the air, trying to maintain the moment that I knew would come crashing down much too quickly. At the bottom of the hill, chest heaving, I'd simply look up into the sky and say thank you for that moment, as time gathered itself back up and started ticking again.

Face flushed with anticipation, I'd pat my pocket to make sure my cookie was secure, and I'd trudge back up the slope again. As I peered down into the void I'd say, "I probably shouldn't do this." Then I launched myself off yet again into space, remorseless and laughing, flying down the slope, potent, strong, as free as an eagle, not knowing yet as a child, that even for the eagle, all space can still be a cage.

That's the snow I long to remember. Looking up into the heavens, I would try to see where it originates, watching the slow fall of it, parachutes of white dropping down, slower and slower. They fall, weightless, ethereal creations of magic and inter-molecular forces, some felled by warmth, some turning to water against one's tongue, some slain by a sled. Yet tomorrow, next year, there would be another flake and yet another and another soul to hold in the palm of their hand, if they are only there to reach out for it.

Barkley continued his play, forever a puppy, with no concept of another winter, only this one, everything just captured here now, running as hard as he could. Looking at a pile of mail on the table to be reviewed, bills to be paid, I wished I could do that, could play in that slow, suspension of time and moisture, one where what you feel and seek and love builds upon itself in endless form, honed by the cold depths of the sky. You can't catch the snow, you can only watch it fall to you, grasping it briefly, stretching out your hands to clasp a wisp of air and hold it for a moment.

But I couldn't, I had obligations and chores and things to do that didn't involve a dog. He barked with a "come follow me" note, but getting chilled just opening the door to check on him, I simply flung his favorite toy as hard and far out into space as I could before I shut the door and impatiently fetched a treat to get him back inside in a few minutes.

"The Toy." It's this bone length thing covered with yellow tennis ball material to which a thick plastic cord is attached so you can really wind it up and throw it. It's *the* toy. He had a half dozen similar shaped toys, but once this one showed up they were ignored. He knows the word "toy" as opposed to "Ball" or "Mr. Squeaky" or "The Ropers" and will fetch it from anywhere, digging through the snow if necessary to find it.

I went into the kitchen, leaving the glass outer door closed, but the curtains opened. Dogs can get frostbite on their paws, ears, and tail if left out in freezing temperatures for lengths of time, so I would keep an eye on him.

I saw this movement in my peripheral vision, a black form jumping up into the air like a kangaroo. What in the. . . . .?

The toy was stuck high up in the branches of a tree, just inside his fenced area, I threw it too far out and too high.

He jumped and he jumped, as if he could somehow magically get that high and grab it. Come on, this next time, surely I'll get it! But he is totally silent, not a bark, so intent on the capture, he is bound and gagged by his obligation.

With a heavy sigh as I'd just gotten warm again, I bundled up in coat and boots and went out. The snow shower had passed, and I could see him out at the edge of the yard, inside the fence that blocked him from the pond. When he saw me, he ceased jumping but continued to stare up. It's just a toy, I thought, but he looked at it as if stuck on the edge of a vast ambiguity, a lonely figure waiting by a hopeless ocean for time and tide to change course.

I've seen many expressions on this dog's face, but this was the first time I could detect "worry." I did not think dogs worried. They don't have taxes, cellulite, ex-spouses or bills; and facial hair as they get older is, well, normal. But they do know hurt; they just quietly take it in, recording it complacently in their suffering, not wishing their person to worry about them.

But today, he looked with a stillness that dropped like stone to the depths of my being, a look on his face that would have stopped even the most involved soul. Dogs can do that, those looks, that put out of mind all of the follies of dog farts, the hair that covers every surface of the house, spent dollars and the chewed shoes. It's a look that made me want to comfort him, even as he does for me with no memory of my failures or the hints of my doubts.

If he could only talk he'd say "Mom, Mom, my toy, she's stuck, help!"

If I fell out there, and broke something I was going to freeze to death. I had stuff to do; this could wait until it's warmer. The ladder was in the garage and the sky was getting dark. All of those thoughts ran through my head as he stared up, my form the only thing between him and that gaping ocean. It's my responsibility. He's my responsibility. But there's no way I was going to try and drag the ladder out of the garage, around the house and through the little gate. I climbed trees as a kid; I only needed to get up a few feet where I could grab the toy or swat it to the ground.

Those childhood trees were stouter trees, however, and I was smaller then, and soon I was half tangled in the young tree, its trunk bending painfully in ways I had not seen since my first Yoga class. I thought of a trebuchet, the laws of physics and how a flung redhead taking out the kitchen window might not be something the insurance agent wanted to hear.

I went and got the ladder. The conquest of worlds, the emancipation of those sold into bondage, the pride and power of freedom's forces, those are fit materials for a courageous tale. The rescue of a fuzzy toy would hardly be accountable but for the look of this dog, for whom the act was as all important, all consuming, as well, bacon will be for me tomorrow morning. This dog had his needs, and I knew that whether I was simply "what's her name with a ladder" or his instrument of documented destiny, I had a role to play here.

Barkley 1. Tree 0.

And the world began revolving again, and I could go back where it was warm, even if I was met with yet another pleading look. Play with me!

"Sorry, buddy, Mom's busy," I said, as I headed back to the garage, leaving that pleading look behind. Overhead, a flock of geese flew past, winging through an aberration of white, a mournful honk, black and white, braving the cold, pursuing the echo of sanctuary. I heard their cry as "come follow me." But I can't. Not quite yet. The snow bloomed with the insistence of spring, and I was earthbound with things to do. I turned away from him, flakes gathered at my feet, tumbled in the wind like rose petals blown aside in a lover's hasty departure.

I still have an evening ahead of me things to do, artifacts of life on my desk, mail to review and bills to pay. On that desk are battered shells and bone, and intertwined with the broken pieces of a black feather from a bird, a pine cone, a small piece of swirled gemstone that looks at me like an eye, daring me to look deeper, to find some closure for those that need it, even if that is me. It was easy to get caught up in that; it's my work, it's how I think, and finding logic to behavior in science that doesn't seem to exist in the human world.

Then there was this goofy dog outside with a fuzzy yellow toy in his mouth, which is covered in snow like it's some ice cream bar. He's simply enjoying the day for what it is. I cannot help but break out in a big grin when I think of that. Perhaps, I'm not as grown up as I think I am.

When the ladder was put away, I turned around and went back toward where I think he wandered. His paw prints that followed me to the gate have already been covered with new snow, his presence but a dream. I closed my eyes for a moment and the paw prints were as if they were never there, a dream that one wakes up smiling from, but can never get back, even if they return to slumber. But he is here. Somewhere. There, a sudden revelation of black fur in the fleeting gleams of snow, with a bark "you came!" that was like the glow of sparks from a struck stone, the wag of a tale which for him is absolute truth. How I will always remember the sound of his barking as I approached, muffled in snow, hearing it as a child, through ear muffs.

I went to him with a pat and a treat, to get him back to the house, to play with me inside in the warmth, while my chores waited for another time. Our feet barely touched the ground as we ran toward the house, toward the gilded blaze, our future, he and I, somewhere ahead in that diffused glow. Like those horses out in the neighbor's field, we moved toward the light of the door, bright as tossed coins in a collection plate, a saving, golden Grace. Home. It is benediction and absolution, even if covered in dog hair.

There is a door, and we fall in, into the embrace of warmth, flakes of cold in dark hair.

23

Moving On

It was time to move, and my friends MC and Mr. B offered to help. I was ready for it. I'd been sleeping on a futon at friends' while the little ranch house showed and closed and that was appreciated. But it was someone else's place, an unfamiliar bathroom, and kids and dogs and noise I wasn't used to. I occasionally provided some entertainment with a "why did you wash your hair with the dog shampoo that was under the sink?" (Dang it, that's the first time my hair's been really soft and shiny). But I was ready to move onward. I could buy another home but I was in no rush and was going to rent for a while, a small place by myself.

The rental thing didn't work out quite as planned but was going to be fun. A female friend had sold her large house quicker than expected and was renting a small place until her retirement a year away when she would move out of state to join her family. She would not mind a roommate, and I suddenly needed a place to live.

I put most of my stuff in storage for now, but for bedroom

and bath items. Barkley and I settled in easily, both of us having spent time here before, which meant Barkley just came on in like he owned the place, a toy rope in his mouth like a flag, claiming the couch for Spain or Spaniels, whatever it is dogs do.

But Barkley did miss his big yard, and my friends who helped me move extended an invite to come up to their house out in the country when we had a free weekend.

We did, thoroughly enjoying multiple trips up there, Barkley playing to his heart's content with their older female black lab named Schmoo. She treated Barkley like some over-testosteroned and slightly goofy friend, gently rebuffing him when she was tired and he wanted to continue to play

Their home had become like one of my own as our friendship grew and Barkley had such a good time up there, with the country to run around in and an assortment of wildlife at which he could bark. It was a part of the state where I could see building a little retirement home someday. But for now, I was content to rent, as Barkley and I spent our weekends exploring and spending time with friends, undecided as to where we wanted to make a home that I hoped was permanent.

One friend I had not seen for a while was my friend EJ. "Seen" is not literal as we'd only chatted on-line with the occasional phone call, for a couple of years now. But we had not met in person, even as many years as we corresponded. I knew a member of his family, so it was as if I'd known him a long time, through their stories, our chats simply reinforcing that. We lived only a couple hundred miles apart, but we were seldom in the same place at the same time it seemed, or he had a girlfriend and was busy.

But this weekend, I got a phone call from him as I was leaving to go back home from Mr. B's house. EJ had been overseas on a project for quite a long time, the casual girlfriend not sticking around, and he was near my hometown for the day after visiting a classmate from college who was getting married.

He said, "I'm in your town; do you have time for coffee? "

"Actually, I've got Barkley and I'm driving down from up North, we could meet halfway. Is that a problem?"

"No," he replied, "I'd love to finally meet Barkley!"

We picked a small restaurant that was along our mutual route, where we could sit out with Barkley and enjoy the pleasant temperatures that day.

I recognized him immediately, and Barkley gave that big goofy grin and tail wag that greets anything friendly that is either on two legs or made of bacon. With a quick hug and a brief walk for Barkley in the grass behind the restaurant, we found some seats and ordered our beverages, while Barkley curled up for a little nap in the breeze.

We'd only intended to stay for a few minutes, both of us having a long drive ahead, and things to do. But we ended up talking for over a couple of hours. You would think that, after all of the previous conversations and his growing up twenty some years after I did, we'd have little to talk about. But the time flew by discussing Lucas Wiring and dogs and airplanes and steam gauges and further debate on how the model of train at the end of movie 3:10 to Yuma was wrong given the year it was supposed to be. You know, important stuff.

I hated to go, but Barkley was growing restless to get home, so we said our goodbyes, planned on meeting up again as friends for a steam engine show in a few weeks. With black labs in the countryside and a guy who likes machinery and dogs, this turned out to be a pretty good weekend.

24

I Left You a Gift

We all come home to different environments. For some, it's the sound of little kids squealing with delight that Mommy or Daddy is home. It's the clatter of footsteps like the thunder of small ponies down a trail that is no trail, but is a hallway rug, worn by that repeated motion of sheer joy.

For some, it's the greeting of a spouse, a friend, or simply the welcoming bark of a dog.

And sometimes what follows is the blissful sound of silence after a really long day. At such times, all you want to do is eat a hot meal and have a mug of hot tea while you lay out the thoughts of the day in your favorite spot to write or perhaps watch one of your favorite old adventure movies.

The night in question was the writing kind, but it was going to be one of those very nights when the tea was a glass of Malbec and the house was totally quiet.

As on most nights, Barkley usually greeted me at the back door to the garage, alerted by the door going up, with that terrifying bark that to outsiders sounds ferocious. He sounded scary, but he'd let me take a bone right out of his mouth with my bare fingers. I'm his protector and his protected and if I want it, it's mine. But he'll defend to the death that bone, from any creature that would harm what he loves. So even with that quiet temperament that is his nature, I know he'd defend to the death, as well, my safety.

But he knows the sound of my truck now, and the barks take on a different tone. I normally hear him before the door is even up, the sound, wild and faint, and incomprehensible, but for its meaning. Bark! Bark! "Mom's Home!"

It was later than normal and when I came in - silence. He was comfy on the couch, Brinks Barkley, sleeping on the job.

I petted him, fed him, and let him out to go potty, which he always does after he eats. I was glad his tummy was feeling OK, as the previous evening he had gobbled up a bit of greasy food wrapper that had hit the floor when I emptied the trash, and I figured that might upset his tummy. But he seemed fine, just not as lively as usual.

Then I poured the wine, put some barley soup on to heat for supper, and sat down to call my friend EJ from the couch.

We had just said hello when I exclaimed "Oh, Crap! Barkley threw up in the corner earlier! I have to go!"

Everyone knows Barkley has an ultra sensitive stomach as far as rawhides and some people foods, unlike a family black lab which could eat a tank and then just gently burp. Even so, several times a year, Barkley snagged some fatty food that's dropped (bacon!) or a piece of sandwich left unattended. He then usually threw it up. He always upchucked in the same spot, if he could not alert me in time that he needed to go out, the corner of the front room between a sofa and chair. Since there's nice carpeting there, I laid out a large, clean towel on it, just in case. But he hadn't had any people food, so I wasn't sure what made him upchuck this time.

Unfortunately, it wasn't barf; it was from the other end. Poor thing.

I'm sure he tried to hold it, but couldn't. He'd never done that in the house since his first couple of weeks home as a puppy. Of course, this time, he carefully *moved the towel out of the way first* before he tagged my floor with the latest of black lab graffiti (in poop!) But I can see the doggy thought process - "Mom gets upset if I grab her clean towels off the counter so I will protect her clean towel even in my indisposition - I'm a good dog!"

He just looked at me from a distance, as if he expected a scolding, as I cleaned it up (pointing out the large area of tile by the front door he could have selected instead of the carpeting, though he didn't appear to be taking notes). There is nothing quite like the look of a dog that's expecting harsh words, no different from a human that somehow knows you are angry, even if they aren't quite sure what exactly they did wrong; a sort of shocked and unbelieving sorrow.

You look at them, your heart beating strongly with the heat of the moment. They look at you, their heart beating a hollow echo as though already retreating, as they wait for your reaction. You look at them again, weighing a hundred expedients, knowing what you need to do, and not necessarily what fatigue and emotion might prod you to do.

I went over and gently scratched his ear saying "It's OK, you couldn't help it, you're a good dog," patted him one last time, and gave my friend a call back.

"It wasn't barf."

He responded, "Oh, so the 'Oh Crap' was literal then?" We laughed and proceeded to chat while Barkley lay down next to me for an ear scratch, feeling fine physically, but needing the reassurance that all was well.

Everyone keeps telling me I need to find a boyfriend now that I'm settled into a new city and job. I wondered if I could meet someone with a carpet cleaning business.

25

The Great Knee Caper

It was supposed to be a perfect weekend. A first visit to my friend EJ's house. After the autumn of outings our friendship was evolving into a bond that knew not the span of years or miles between us.

He was inviting a few of his friends over to meet me. I had a new outfit; Barkley was going to be on his best behavior. All his friends would like me. There would be crème brulee that had absolutely *no* calories.

So how did I end up in an MRI machine, after two days in his easy chair with a pack of frozen peas on my knee?

Take one black lab, excited for a walk after a long drive. Add an icy set of steps and a female golden retriever across the street. The fact that the vet rendered him incapable of knowing exactly what to do with a female did not deter him. He lunged to greet her at the same moment my knee turned ninety degrees to go the other way and my center of gravity, always far forward anyway, was pointed the wrong way.

The doctor at the emergency room said, "You likely have a torn meniscus, you will need an orthopedic specialist and an MRI."

It was two days before Christmas. My doctor was two hundred miles away and EJ was planning on going home to see his family for the holiday. My roommate was also out of town for Christmas and New Years. But I was in too much pain to travel for a couple of days, even if I could have driven myself.

Christmas itself was subdued, myself in pain and feeling bad about ruining his holiday. But we made the best of it, opening gifts, setting the 60s aluminum tree and matching color wheel briefly out on the covered porch. That, of course, resulted in comments that we should not have the color wheel out there on a final approach to an airport, due to the dangers of pilots being blinded by bright laser lights.

"Captain! There's a bright light in my eyes! It's Green. Wait it's Blue, now it's Orange, now it's Red!"

Even as much as I hurt, I laughed, with a vision of law enforcement showing up to confiscate the color wheel and we made the best we could of our Christmas.

With driving out of the question for me, EJ cancelled everything and drove me back to my place, an appointment made to get an MRI and an orthopedic consult.

That first night home Barkley stayed glued to my side. There was nothing to do but wait as serene and still as possible, while others did the worrying for me. Outside, the moon shone on nibbled shadow, the only other lights as far off and distant as memories of shame or pride or loss, remembered there with a sharp twinge of the knee, then fading to dim memory as Barkley leaned into me with a comforting snuggle.

The MRI was done the next day, the news confirming that I would need surgery, and right away.

Barkley hovered with that worried concern that dogs can convey, he more so than most, with Groucho Marx eyebrows that could move up and down with the most expressive of facial expressions.

He wasn't the only one hovering.

EJ canceled a business trip and stayed with me through the surgery and the first week of recovery, cooking for me, helping me up and down and making sure Barkley was fed and exercised.

I was not the best of patients, not wanting to take the pain meds, other than that first day, so as not to feel loopy.

I was also anxious to get out of the house. I hated the crutches, but at least they were so big Barkley could not get them in his mouth and carry them around like the cane.

After a week, EJ needed to get back to work and we confirmed I could manage on my own. An old exercise step had a hole drilled through it with a cord that attached to my truck's head rest. I could drop it on the ground; step in, then pull it up, the truck too tall for me to manage otherwise.

I got checked out on the scooters at the local stores, until such time as I could ditch the crutches.

The scooter was fun, though one of the greeters came over and asked if I needed help operating the controls (consisting of forward, backward, right and left). Granted, it might be more difficult than a jet aircraft, but I was good to go, thanking them for their help. Speed wise, it was fair to say the scooters were slower than the INDY 500 and faster than a snail on Demerol. But I was not only able to do a cookie in the chicken aisle; I found that the displays in the electronic section made for great S patterns at top speed. I also discovered that large guys with carts containing a hundred bags of Tater Tots and beer can move surprisingly fast when faced with a redhead in a Springfield Armory T-shirt, converging at top scooter speed.

Dealing with the crutches and the scooter was the hardest part. I tried holding them, but that made it hard to work the controls. I put one out front. Jousting – Big Box Mart Style (if you can knock a Billy Bass out of someone's cart with it, it's bonus points). I finally gave in and let EJ carry them while I tried to burn rubber doing .02 mph, keeping watch that the store manager was not involved in radar trail tactics.

I also set up a schedule of friends to come over and walk Barkley for a few weeks. He'd been great, viewing the whole crutch thing as a human equivalent of "the Cone of Shame," looking at me with pity for my having to use them, and convincing me that his body heat would be the only thing keeping me from freezing to death there in my big bed.

Before EJ leaves, I will make us a dinner of pancakes, if I can keep upright long enough to cook.

When I was a kid we'd have pancakes for Sunday breakfast, but sometimes we'd have them for dinner as well. It was usually when the household budget was tight. My Mom quit her seventeen-year career as a LEO to be a full time Mom, and Dad took a lesser paying position that allowed him to be home every night, sacrifices I know that made a difference in our lives. Certainly I remember those dinners and the laughter and the love that lived in the house 24/7, more than any brand new bike I didn't get.

We'd have different toppings for them, maple syrup and lingonberry jam, perhaps some real butter from a nearby farm and a little molasses.

As we ate, Dad would finally relax after a long stressful day at work, and we'd tell the tales of our day and small childhood victories. For these breakfasts at dinner, no worries about money, or the mortgage or the future. Simply bites of life shared with those you love. I'd savor one bite, even while anticipating the next, the golden disks disappearing like coins well spent.

Tonight, I toss one plain one like a Frisbee, as I give my knee a rest, caught in the mouth of a dog that's shown nothing but patience. Like pancakes for dinner, such was this Christmas, unexpected, not ending as planned, but full of little bits of sweetness and caring from those that are becoming like family.

26
Resolutions

Recovery from the knee surgery went about as well as could be, considering I was missing about fifteen percent of the meniscus. Physical therapy was going well, and I only needed the cane for steps.

I remember when I got home from the hospital. Barkley was waiting, coming up and sniffing my leg, as if he could somehow tell something was different. But as dogs instinctively do, he knew I didn't feel well and quietly waited there on his bed, until I got settled into my own and EJ could take him for a long walk.

We'd missed New Years Eve, not that I had planned anything. In years past I had often spent such holidays on call or working, maybe taking a glance at my watch if I was still awake at midnight. Elsewhere thousands of people would gather, as if the whole slumbering stroke of midnight which they could not yet see beyond or past--would somehow pass them by, should they look away, missing that final count.

It seems I often end up working on such holidays, the forces of man and nature in a hurry to come to some unspoken conclusion that ends with my hustling around out in the cold, the dance of a woman gathering up a string of broken pearls in a burning house. There's a frantic patience in such work, and time usually slips past; my only awareness that the work is done is the gentle chiding of birds in the trees, the sound of a metal door closing.

At such times my only resolution is simply to get home again, the only promise that of the brief death of sleep that was in itself, the end, the escape, and my reward.

But this time, there was no keeping with the typical New Year's resolution for two days, then locating the nearest Dunkin Donuts. If I was going to get back to full use of this knee, I had to do my therapy, keep up with my exercises and get back walking as soon as the doctor said I was ready. If left to my own devices, I might be tempted to just curl up with a book, but Barkley was counting on me to get well so he could get out of the house as he needed to.

The first weeks were tough; it was all I could do just to maneuver around the home or work while friends walked Barkley. Since I could not yet walk him on a leash, for fear of an "I've fallen and can't get up" moment, I engineered a line out into the backyard so I could hook him up to go out into the unfenced grass without fear of him getting into the road.

By early spring I was done with physical therapy and ready to start walking regularly again. I didn't have my entire knee, but I'd have my black furry "petometer," who made sure I got out at least twice a day to walk, even if a friend held the leash for me as we walked those first few days. But I still had two sturdy legs and today I was going to try them out and see if I could jog a bit. I had to leave Barkley behind for just a few more days, until I was sure I could do this, but I was going to try.

With that look on his face that says "You're going without me?" I scurried from the house, through the cold down to the train tracks and over to that little church whose vestry of which is so old it appears unpainted—its pale and weathered appearance from a distance appearing to be part of the stern and silent road. Behind it, sat a small cemetery, the stones, old and plain, with no markings or decorations, only a name and dates. It was as if all the mourners remembered of them to carve was simply a name and those dates or the fact that the obliteration of a human life was so often so simple and so final that the verbiage which encloses it had to be almost monotonous in its display: "I was here, then on this day I wasn't. Next!"

So I turned around, and I marched back toward home and Barkley, reminding myself that I was alive, feeling strong and invincible, the brace of life flowing in and out of my lungs, feeling every bit of my body, there under the clothes. I could do this! My body is that of a warrior, the extra twenty pounds, the little used muscles, my enemy. Barkley barked at the triumphant warrior's return. Biscuits for everyone!

Then I woke up the next day and discovered that not only

had my enemy not retreated from the field, it had stolen my weapons. I thought I had stormed the castle and instead found myself in an unholy alliance with the enemy, who reminded me with every single movement of its superiority, as it mocked with nerve endings I'd forgotten I had.

Everything hurt, even my hair. Barkley was looking at me, holding his leash in his mouth. It was so cold outside. I did *not* want to do this again this morning. But I did, for one of the resolutions I will stick with is ensuring that this creature with which I share a life has the care he needs, the motion that keeps him happy and healthy. That is a resolution I can stick with. For him, I will.

Such it is with things that we make a decision to change; something that may benefit us, something that may simply benefit someone we love. It may not happen in a day, or even a month. But it will happen.

Yes, it will happen. It might be that decision to put behind us that which hangs silent and brooding in the dark vault of our regret. It might be that moment in which we grow up, which can happen at sixteen years of age, at thirty or even sixty, assuming that clock of responsibility, that intimation of our willingness to carry our own weight, and in doing so, holding our head up high, for those decisions which by virtue of our adulthood, are our own to make.

That is resolve, not a New Year's Resolution, but a way in which I would live each day, taking good care of myself, so I could care for this four-legged companion. For he had never once said, "It's too cold" or "I'm too tired" when I've needed the encouragement of a dog's wagging tail.

My knee still hurt. And it would for a while, but I still had time. The day wouldn't be over until tomorrow, even as it began a thousand years ago. In every day will be an instant that is history; one that can't be glimpsed yet, for what we are seeing may have its meaning a year from now, but not today. Today is my day, and I can either turn back now or retreat into the past, or sail conclusively on, towards the world's brilliant rim.

I'd choose the journey onward, as I grabbed a leash and pulled up those sweat pants over aching muscles. I may go slower than on day one, but assuredly would make my path down to the railroad tracks, over to the church, thinking not of miles or muscles, but of weathered lumber, the simple crossroads of mortality and the conclusion of flesh, thankful for each moment that I was alive and not alone. Even the moments that hurt.

27

I Feel Like Someone Is Staring at Me

The roommate situation was going well. I was saving money and paying off debts without a mortgage, including that last student loan for grad school that I was certain I'd be paying off until I was dead. I was having fun looking at houses for sale in the paper, and assorted plans, perhaps to build one of my own.

My roommate was gone every weekend, visiting her family, and I had the place to myself. During the work week, we were often on different shifts and wouldn't see each other but for a brief greeting as we passed each other in the hall.

We were both neat, keeping the place spotless but for the dog hair. We also both enjoyed the same TV shows, picking apart the science and procedures in most cop shows and laughing at all the female lawyers and forensic specialists who went around wearing skin tight, plunging designer tops and high heels. That's certainly going to make sure you're taken seriously, we'd laugh, as Barkley jumped up to catch a dog treat.

The layout of the house was such that my bedroom was on the opposite end from her room, so I did not wake her up, or vice versa. It was working well. But she had never been around dogs.

Mind you, she loved Barkley, having been my friend for several years, but she wasn't used to doggie behavior. He, as well, wasn't used to having two people around.

"Whose sock do I steal? Is it the first one home, is it the newest one? Maybe I can just stuff them ALL in my mouth." More than once she had to wrestle an item of clothing from him, probably losing a stocking or two in the process but never complaining.

He also doubled the begging, and I found out he was getting extra treats when she came home, then acting like he was starving after she'd gone to bed early for a morning shift, and I was rolling in.

There was also the matter of possessions. Barkley and I had declared detente on throw pillows and kitchen towels.

But my roommate had a doll collection--those really expensive ones that look like they are alive. When she was gone, the door to her room where they were lined up around the wall was closed, because frankly, having their eyes on me as I watched TV down the hall was creepy. In addition, if the door was open, I could picture Barkley snagging $100 worth of curls and pinafores and running through the house with it like his tail was on fire.

Not a good way to keep a roommate.

So I got a baby gate, that way he could stay in my end of the place if I had to run an errand, and I could keep him out of her stuff. Coming home one night, she had already gone to bed and he looked at me with a pitiful glance as I bent over to "release the hounds."

"So Barkley, how many extra treats did you talk our roommate out of?"

As I bent down, I could see something at the corner of his eye, I thought I'd seen the beginning of a little cyst there, but it had gotten bigger. Likely nothing to worry about, but I'd take him to his new vet this week. She was great, and he loved going there. I'm sure she could take care of it.

And I was worried about something else. Even with all the extra treats, he was losing some weight.

28

It's All Fun and Games until Someone Ends Up in a Cone

Dr. H. was able to get us in soon, an appointment first thing in the morning, Barkley being due for a check up anyway. Barkley is probably the only dog I've ever known that *likes* going to the veterinarian. He's as excited as if their front door was opening up to the Frozen Yogurt Shop and he was going to get the world's biggest cup (and no, you can't have gummy bears as a topping).

"Oh Boy! It's the Vee E Tee! New People! Cat Smells!"("And no, Barkley, you don't get to wear a little paper gown").

I hoped this would be something simple and that little growth near his eye could be easily removed.

Dr. H. and an assistant looked at him in the little exam room we waited in and then took him from me to another room. I heard a meowing (cat scan??) somewhere and then nothing for a while. I imagine this is a bit like what a parent feels when they have a child who is sick, trying to put on a strong front, so the little ones do not sense it, but scared underneath for things that one has no control over.

I step out into the hall, so no one notices a tear. Dawn still lays upon the horizon, the sun pushing back a somber wall of darkness, the eastern sky lighting up in crimson and gold and the Pentecostal red of fire. It is light that makes the water seep further from my eyes, closing them, wishing only for the comforting hue of black, warm fur against my face. Up above hangs a solitary cloud, leaving a single shadow on the earth, all alive, and so very alone.

I went back into the little exam room to sit and wait.

Dr. H. came back to talk to me. "It's a tumor," she gently said. She also quickly added that the type is usually benign, though we'd already discussed that black labs are the breed that can get the more wicked kind. Based on what she sees when it is removed, it will be examined histopathologically. I've got the best vet in the area, very talented and concerned for her patients and their families so I know he's in good hands and I'm hoping it's one of the benign ones.

He's scheduled for surgery on Thursday after a bunch of screenings to ensure, with his age, he gets the proper sedation. They gave me the estimate of the cost. I looked down at the written form. Lab fee after lab fee. "I should have gotten a different breed," I say to the receptionist, and she's kind enough to laugh at my bad joke, knowing I'm trying to remain upbeat.

But money is not the object, his well-being is.

The surgery was soon done, and he was home from the Animal Hospital. Barkley was still pretty out of it from the meds (look, a squirrel . . . . zzzzzzz). Dr. H. had told me during the exam earlier in the week that the tumor was likely a meibomian gland adenoma, benign or other type of benign neoplasm. Those are common in older dogs and though I don't think of Barkley as old, he is over seven now. If it's not, she could tell that when she cut into it. But based on what she saw during the excision, she was sending it out to a pathologist. We should have the histopathology report to indicate the type of tumor and mitotic rate soon.

Until then, it was just rest, prayer and the Cone of Shame. He had no idea why I would put such an evil contraption on him, looking at me with this profound surprise. It's as if he is the punch line of a joke he does not get, and there is nothing I can do for him to make him understand. Though he was only allowed on the bed on special occasions, I fixed up a spot for him on the twin bed in the office where he could look out the window and make up a nest of travel beds and pillows on the floor so he could get some sleep with the cone on.

He didn't like it, but he managed to secure a sock and two pot holders, all while wearing the cone, spending the rest of his time staring out the window like the old RCA dog, listening for something that even dogs can't hear.

I wasn't sure if either of us was getting much rest, but soon, the pathology report was in. It was not good news, but it could be worse.

It was cancer and a malignant sort but distant metastasis is very uncommon in this one: Meibomian Epithelioma. Basically, it's a tumor of low-grade malignancy arising from the meibomian glands (modified sebaceous glands which are located on the inner surface of the eye). Dr. H. has only seen one in her many years of practice. The pathologist said the abnormal cells had spread to the margins so it could come back. He was doing better now (though when I left the room he probably surfed the web for C4, a shovel and articles about Cone disposal) and would probably eat more and gain back some weight when he felt better. But the first six months after surgery are crucial and constant monitoring is a must. That is something I could do. I do not love very often, but I love hard, and this dog had got more than a bit of my heart.

After twelve days, the Cone of Shame was finally gone, and we'd be able to travel in the truck up to see our friend EJ soon. The report was back on his lymph nodes and all was clear. That was great news! Barkley was happier though, about getting rid of the cone. What would Barkley do with this newly found freedom?

"Barkley, don't lick yourself there!"

29

Dogs and Cats Living Together

Words can do our bidding, but sometimes nothing else will.

Especially a cat.

I went for some years before Barkley without a dog, believing with my life and schedule and commitments I just didn't need one. But I never had cats.

Suddenly, as Barkley came into my life and we opened our world to a lot more than work, I met a lot of other animal people, and many of them had cats. Fortunately, Barkley stayed with a friend for a few weeks when he was a pup, when I was traveling and his regular dog sitter was having surgery. It was a comfortable country home that came with an assortment of dogs, cats, and grandkids, and he had a grand time with them.

The cats I was around now belong to my friends, MC and Mr. B. There is Tank, oh, so aptly named, the one that sleeps with me every night when I visit them. Then there is lovable Bob, a big yellow Nerf ball with legs, as well as Socks and Goldie. Our visits with them included Barkley and their black lab Schmoo just hanging out, lots of food and fun times, EJ joining us when he could. Knowing MC was like having a sister, and Mr. B was not just a fabulous cook, he was an engineer like EJ, so they got along great, and those were times I looked forward to.

I was still residing in a rental home, not feeling rushed to buy something else, undecided on whether I wanted to buy a small house close to work, or a small place in the country. Due to job transfers and family circumstance, Barkley and I had moved three times in his lifetime and I was tired of moving. Besides, the money would accrue more interest in investments other than the current real estate market, which for me had proven about as economically sound as tossing my money off of a building.

Since both Barkley and I were somewhat housing unencumbered, my friends with the four cats, needing to both be out of town for a few days, asked me to housesit. I had some vacation time I could use and would love to be out in the country, so I said yes and Barkley and I arrived. We'd be fine on our own for a few days, EJ planning to come over on a couple of evenings to visit and help out as needed.

The house sitting was going pretty well I thought, after that first couple of days. Six animals in the house kept me busy, but there were many hours to read or write (or sit with a Big Orange Cat in my lap while I watched the Rifleman on big screen TV). I'd handled the litter box for four cats well (thank you, surgical mask!)

I might not even need EJ's help, though part of me wished for his company. The house was quiet; all the animals were snoozing, and all was right with the world. As it got dark, the lights off, I sensed movement from the master bedroom across the hall, where Barkley and a couple of cats were napping.

Barkley whined. It was a soft plaintive whine, not of pain, just of worry. I heard him moving, toward me, but he was not moving fast.

Another whine as he entered the hall that was lit.

He had been on the bed of my friends, the top coverlet a crocheted type. The little hook of his rabies tag had caught in it. Of course, with multiple pets trying to nest in it, it was wrapped up in all the covers, which he was now trying to run down the hall with it in tow. Lying on the tail end of all of it was Bob the Cat, riding it like a travois.

Barkley was unhooked; Bob was displaced (much to his displeasure) with only minimal blood loss on my part and the bed was remade.

I called for backup though.

There were some things I learned about cats that week. To start, out in the country, no matter how many cats are in the house, mice will still come in when it dips down into the low 30s at night. Even though all four cats were peering out the window, the mice would come in, a suicide mission if there ever was one.

I also discovered that four cats, defying all laws of physics and thermodynamics, can, on a daily basis, turn 36 ounces of basic sustenance into 16 pounds of poop. Outside of politics I've not seen a conversion quite like it.

I also found that cats can be so much fun—except for the morning I had to clean up a stain the size of Vermont where Goldie horked up what appeared to be William Shatner's toupee.

Still, as much as those critters are family, I am a "dog person." I love how dogs wait, they long for your return and greet you with an unbridled joy that knows no bounds. On those days that I came home drained from a difficult day, tears in my eyes and the worry of ghosts in my soul, Barkley was there. Barkley simply laid his head on my knee and looked up, as if that moment is what he lived for. His tail would wag with a healing that humans can't always give.

He didn't care how new or fancy his house was, what he rode in, or what collar he wore. All he cared about was how to bequeath that which sustains him, in his too short life: his faith and his love, as he patiently waited, only wanting me to come back into the room where he lay.

But I admire how that when I was away, he was fine, bonding with friends who care for him, some related by blood, some just related by love and friendship. Unlike most cats, which just have staff, dogs have their pack, and Barkley had his own among my friends.

They cared for him as did I. Once while I was away, he injured a leg, jumping high for a toy, just like he always did, one minute happy, the next, hobbling with pain. My friends were beyond concerned, and we hoped it was just a sprain. When I got home, he was a little better, and then quit eating, then drinking, and my concern turned to panic.

I called my friend, Tam, and she came over, helping me make a little stretcher out of a rug to get him into the truck and off to an animal hospital in the city that was open on a Sunday. It was a simple soft tissue injury where he'd overextended his leg, and they kept him overnight for some hydration, some pain and anti-inflammatory meds and he was better. But I was like a parent there in the waiting room, the young male vet trying to soothe me as I fought tears. He said, "Are you by yourself?" and I sniffed, "No, a friend is with me." He said, "I'll go find them, what do they look like?"

I said, "Look for the beautiful six-foot-tall, pony-tailed blond in the ball cap pacing the lobby looking worried." That young man was quite happy to share the news.

I understand. When I blew my knee out, in a city far away, needing surgery, not even able to drive my own truck home to my own doctor, my best friend took care of me.

That is what family has always done, and pets are our family. But although you can own a dog, he's with you because he wants to be. Short of tying him up, if Barkley was truly unhappy here he could just jump the fence and leave in a heartbeat, off to the land of unlimited biscuits and Moms who don't live out of a suitcase part of the year. He is bound only by choice, not vow or ring or law.

But he did not leave. Each day, be it rain, shine, or snow, he was here for me, even if I was not present. That was his gift to me, one I accepted gladly for as long as he lived.

30

Problems in the End Zone

There weren't many dogs in my neighborhood. There was a home behind me in which lived what could be either a great lumbering dog or a Shetland pony. I only saw it when I was out the door before 5:00 a.m. and I was half asleep, the owner walking him on a lead out into the mist. A couple of homes down was a little yappy dog of mixed heritage that looked like a big Twinkie with legs. The owners sometimes let her out to do her business without a leash and sometimes she wandered to visit the neighbors, though she knew to stay out of the street. Barkley mostly ignored her, and they had a relationship of distrust and mutual avoidance except when there was a camera out, much like some Hollywood marriages.

Barkley *was* the king of the block; however, this morning he was sleeping on a twin bed near my computer after an interesting night of "guess what I ate."

That's why he didn't get people food except as a very small and infrequent treat such as plain roast chicken, bits of cheddar, or frozen peas (he loves them, nibbling them from your bare fingers like little ball bearings). He's not particular, but he'll seek out the smallest crumb if left unattended.

Last night he and I were home alone, my roommate off and home with her family, her retirement looming. Barkley snagged something off the counter when I was out of the room briefly, licking his lips as I returned; while my piece of homemade pizza looked clearly disturbed and rather lacking in a sage infused sausage. Later, I caught him in the garbage looking for more (once they've had a taste…).

But spicy or greasy food and Barkley have never seen eye to eye. He did pretty well, though, other than a couple delicate sage scented burps and one episode where he came in while I was taking my bath. He came in and just sat down with this *look* on his face that clearly said, "*OMG* Mom, what's that *smell*!"

He then turned around and looked at his butt as if it was suddenly possessed.

No words were spoken but what passed between us was this:

"No, Barkley, you cannot put the Menthol Rub in your nostrils, that's Mommy's."

Then the smell hit.

Well, that emptied me out of the tub faster than realizing NCIS starts in thirty seconds. A quick spray of air freshener and an open window and he settled down for the night after leaving a quick calling card on the tree by the garage for the neighbor dog. I had a suspicion that the night was not going to be a calm one.

That was confirmed when I woke up after midnight and realized I'd not closed the garage door. The back door from the garage to inside is heavy and well secured, but I've got a bike and tools in the garage that I would not want stolen.

With only the hall light on; I stepped out into the garage, only to have some furred creature rush out at me from under the truck.

"Son of a . . . !"

Seeing just a soundless flash of fur and tooth, my foot instinctively went out to keep it away from me, catching the creature under the chest with the top of my slipper and tossing it OUT the garage door like some sort of overtime field goal. Georgia against UT couldn't have done any better!

YIP! Yip yip yip yip yip yip.

Oh, no, I just dropped kicked the neighbors' yappy dog. How am I going to explain THAT? I looked out; the dog wasn't out there injured; he headed straight back toward home, the garage door being up a foot or two for him to go in and out. I had not contacted ribs, just sort of propelled him on the top of my shoe out, so I was pretty sure he'd be startled but unhurt. But I'd go see to him in the morning to make sure he was OK and explain what happened.

My pulse was still going like Speed Racer. Back to bed, I tossed and turned, heart still racing, hoping the rest of the night and weekend would go better.

All was well until about four a.m. when Barkley stuck his nose in my face (and not to say hello), with the doggie alert of "I gotta go!" I know that panting and that dance, and it means *now*. I threw on something over my pajamas and headed out the garage with him. He made a beeline for the corner of the property; eighty some pounds of muscle pulling me like a Nantucket sleigh ride through the dark, realizing I'm standing out there in a tiny Victoria's Secret polka dot number covered with a Day-Glo yellow first responders coat. Somewhere there's probably a calendar composed of women in outfits like that, but it was not a look I wanted my neighbors to see. "Officer, not only did she drop kick our dog but she goes around dressed as the Village People but half naked."

Barkley wasn't kidding. He didn't just have to *go*.

Remember the Darwin Award where the guy allegedly attached a JATO bottle to the back of a car and it launched him into a cliff?

There are certain circumstances where there is not much difference between a JATO assisted Chevy Impala and a Labrador Retriever digestive tract.

Just saying.

Once emptied, he seemed OK, drank some water and just went back to sleep. At least HE could get back to sleep.

In the morning, I checked on him while I was making some corn muffins for breakfast. He still wasn't too perky, but he was better.

By late morning, I had finished reading a book, and the little yappy dog was happily running around in its front yard, looking none the worse for wear, though it was steering clear of my driveway. Barkley also ate some breakfast and wanted to play with his toy without any further detonation. Hooray!

I think this would call for a little celebration. So after lunch, Barkley and I took a little road trip, not too far, as I had to be ready to go to work if needed, but for one of his favorite treats.

Barkley got a little vanilla frozen yogurt. Mom got a really big one.

31

Marco!

Barkley loves the water, but unfortunately, if he gets into a pond, either with permission or without, he tends to get an ear infection.

He'd not been in the pond lately, but at a time pilots refer to as stupid o'clock, Barkley came to the bedroom door, shaking his head side to side. Jingle, Jingle, as his tags clacked together. "Go back to bed," I said. He stood there and shook his head again, and again, and again. Great, it's OCD (obsessive compulsive dog). I got up and checked to make sure his collar was comfortable, and then checked his ears, as he is prone to ear infections when allergy season is bad, which it was lately. Shake Shake Jingle Jingle. The ear checking involved almost ninety pounds of Labrador retriever twerking and several wrestling holds that would make WWF proud, but it showed some inflammation that wasn't there a couple days ago. So off to the vet we'd go when they opened.

He got some care and medicine at the vet's for his ears to clear them up. Plus he got a treat from each veterinary tech that stopped by to pet him with a "oh, it's a black lab!" as he gave everyone that "No one has given me *anything*" look.

But vet visits can be expensive, and the ear problem is uncomfortable for him, so I needed to find another alternative for water fun in the summer.

While at a Big Box Mart, EJ and I spotted a small kids' pool, about a foot deep and cheap so we got it for him. The top ring of it inflated which then held up the formed plastic liner that shaped the pool. It was pretty small, but we figured he'd have fun with it as he had one some years ago and loved it.

We got it assembled, laughing our heads off at the symbol printed on the pool of a guy diving from a great distance into water with a "no diving" symbol. It's a foot deep!

Once assembled and put in the backyard, Barkley looked at it, gingerly sticking his toe in it, then the whole leg. After that he walked through it, and out, and then ran. Then the big jump and splash.

Unfortunately, he noticed the tasty inflatable ring and bit into it "Look, a Donut!"

Whoosh! Out came the air. So much for that idea.

On a later weekend, I was visiting EJ and walking past the hardware store in his little village, when we spotted a plastic kiddie pool. Solid, one piece plastic. BINGO!

I wasn't sure if it would fit in his car, and for a moment I thought I'd have to carry it home on my back like a turtle, so we went and got my truck and returned for it.

We set it up and filled it. Then we sat out on folding chairs with a cold drink and watched him for a couple hours play in that pool, having to refill the water a couple times. I could not stop smiling as I watched him.

Perhaps it's just the memory of happy childhood times without all the angst and emotions that adults can put in your lap, dragging you down. Perhaps it's just that ebb and flow of water, setting a cadence to the flow of innocence as it is slowly swept away by time, by experience. But later that week, when I was out on the road, I realized it had been too long since I climbed into a pool.

And there I was one night, in a hotel with a pool. I could sit and stare at the walls waiting for seasons to pass in their ordered immortal sequence. I could make origami out of USA Today. There had to be something else to do. This place was too expensive for families with kids, and all the businessmen were having free drinks at happy hour. No one was going to notice if I slipped into the pool in a pair of workout shorts and a T-shirt and swam a few laps.

And I did, watching my shadow on the wall as I did a cannon ball right near the big sign that says, "No diving," watching the water lap against the pool filter outlet as I managed to do an underwater turn, coming up in a butterfly stroke that I thought I'd forgotten.

Marco!

But there was no response.

The water does more than baptize us; it washes us clean; it propels us out on waves of laughter into one buoyant moment when there are no worries. Children are not the only ones to drop their guard in these moments of play, when for a moment the evanescent clutter of an adult life is swept away. So not caring if I was kicked out of the pool for diving or for having a good time, I splashed and cavorted in a pool of water that had the bottomless candor of a child's face. Simple fun without unreasonable expectations, something we adults seem reluctant to grasp. And for the first time in a few long, hot, hard weeks of work, my face emptied of worry--I laughed like a child.

I climbed from the pool, heart pounding from the exercise, and grabbed my towel to head back toward my room. There I climbed into the shower, still clothed, to rinse the chlorine from my workout gear and my hair, letting the water sluice over me until it grew cold. As I stared in the mirror at a wet haired form, I only saw memory. But in memory, I would see my small, wet self there so many years before: short hair, wearing a silly looking swim outfit, and smiling. I may be still as unfashionable as ever, but now I wear my long hair down my back like a red badge of defiance.

I wonder about the next time I jump into the water, not caring what people think. Will I recall at that moment, all those days of freedom, of the smell of lemons in the summer air, the sun on my nose, growing yet another freckle, all the worries of anything other than this moment, washed away? Will I taste the water, clear and smelling ever so faintly of bleach, as it swirled down the drain with all my future tears?

Marco!

The words will ring out like the slap of water against a childhood friend.

Polo!

32

Take this Job and Shovel It.

By having a fenced backyard in my former home, I was relieved to be free of the embarrassment of Barkley finding the perfect place to do "No. 2" in front of someone's dining room window, which occurred regularly in the first neighborhood we lived in together.

Now, I had a rental home that didn't have a fenced backyard and I'd learned to make sure he was "empty" in our own little yard before we got on a walk around the neighborhood.

Having done his business, both barrels, I loaded him up with me to make a long drive to a friend's house northeast of home, to pick up some shelves they were getting rid of now that the kids had moved out. It would be a couple hours round trip, and Barkley is always fun company.

He loved going for a ride in the truck, beside himself if I fired it up without him except in the mornings. He seemed to understand that when I said, "Mom's going to work," and have my gear with me, that he can't go and that I will come back. Any other time, I got that look of panic.

He seemed puzzled that we did not have an overnight bag today. Usually when he went with me it was for a weekend visiting my friends, and there was always a suitcase.

I'd made the drive up north to visit my friends so many times, I could pretty much pinpoint within a five minute window when I'd arrive based on the traffic of the day. I'd learned the best places to stop for a clean restroom, I'd learned that the State Bird of Indiana *is* the Orange Cone and no amount of breath holding, prayer, or curses in bad Gaelic, will make the traffic move any faster.

I'd pretty much given up on getting good gas mileage in the four x four truck, each round trip costing me about a hundred bucks. I'd tried the usual tricks: turning my engine off when at a red light, easing off the gas when going downhill or whenever a song by AC/DC comes on the radio. I'd removed anything that's not aerodynamic; no "We're # 1!" foam finger on the antenna after a Colts game; everything on the vehicle is clean and tight. But it's money well spent—time with people that have become part of my family, not a replacement for it.

Today's drive was easy, but instead of napping, as he usually does, Barkley seemed aware we were going in a different direction, and was trying to stretch every last inch out of his restraint system and get his head up front, to see what was going on. I'd tried to deter him from that as I do not want him whacking my seat with his head if I come to a sudden stop.

Saying "no" to him did not work, he'd just scoot closer. What I found that worked was singing. I inherited the family vocal abilities (all volume, no tone), so launching into a lively Sea Shanty instantly sends him to the back seat.

Whiskey-o, Johny-o
Rise her up from down below
Whiskey, whiskey, whiskey-o
Up aloft this yard must go
John rise her up from down below

Barkley gives me a look that says, "Mom, the engine is making a horrible noise!" and retreats in his harness to the back seat, not even looking forward.

Today was a short drive though, and it was uneventful. We arrived, made polite conversation that involved me remarking on their new siding while Barkley peed on their front Azaleas, loading up the shelves, and leaving a plate of cookies (chocolate chip being the current exchange rate among friends). Then it was back to home. As we neared home, I realized I needed a file from work. It was my day off, but I would need it tomorrow before an early meeting away from the office. Work was open, so I'd just duck in real quick and grab it.

As we pulled in, Barkley started making that whiny sound that I knew meant he had to go potty.

"Can't it wait? We'll be home in ten minutes."

The whining increased, and he started doing that little dance in the back seat of the truck.

"OK, just for a second." There was a grassy area behind the building, a good portion of which was empty space, not leased. I'd get the leash and a bag for clean up and take him out there. I unhooked the seat belt extension from his harness. He *pushed*, almost knocking me over as he was out the door, heading for the grass.

"Barkley, no, your leash!" He ran way past the vacant windows, squatted, and left a large, steaming land mine on the grass.

Right in front of my boss's window.

The scenery of our lives may be in constant motion, but some things never change.

33

The Check Up

As Barkley's birthday approached, it dawned on me it had been a year since his surgery to remove a malignant tumor from the corner of his eye. My roommate had retired and moved, and he and I were settled into the cozy rental all on our own. He was certainly happy to be rid of the "Cone of Shame" but I do not think he realized how worried I was. Afterwards, everything looked clear on the eye, which the vet was able to keep from harm during the delicate surgery and he was getting regular follow up checks.

The confirmation that all was well was his yearly exam and shots last Saturday morning. Just looking at him there in the waiting area, I could see the difference from the last year, when both of us were distressed more than we'd let on.

As he and I waited on the vet, instead of worrying, I could just play with him and talk to him as I always do, as if he could understand me.

"Say Barkley, do you want one of those "Thundershirts" that

Doctor H. has on display?"

Barkley (cocking his head and thinking to himself). "I tried one on, I thought it'd make me look cool like Jim Cantore and chicks would dig me, but they didn't."

He got his booster shots and a thorough exam. His lymph nodes were clear; no parasites anywhere, no heartworm, healthy in every aspect. I'd have to bring him in again in a few weeks for some doggie dental care, but outside of that we were good to go.

Dogs are an expense, they are worry, and time, and hair, and walks in the rain and the cold. They are also part of the everyday fabric of our lives, to the point that when they leave us, we feel the chill.

Our dogs don't care what we wear, where we live, how we vote or who we call our friends, as long as those we surround ourselves with are kind. For they recognize anger, they recognize cruelty, even as they forgive more than any one of us ever would. Dogs don't know the word "love." To them it's just a word like any other, a sound that defines or simply fills a lack, a word they don't need to know any more than they need to know the word for fear and pride. Yet, though they can't articulate it, they show it, as though nothing else had ever been, our form the shape and echo of all that is necessary to them.

I watched him play in a little park in the old part of town, briefly as it was so warm out. So little makes him so happy, random barks, a metronome of a tail, jumping and grabbing his toy with that quality of never-ending hope, the eyes looking at me with a look that is forever ready for mirth. I take the toy and he sits, looking at me with that tentative and abject eagerness of someone for whom there is just one wish, and it's about to be fulfilled.

I own many books on many subjects. Tucked in drawers, not on display, are diplomas and awards, commendations for things I have done, or have applied. No classroom, no flight deck, no laboratory, has taught me more than a dog. A dog has taught me how to look carefully and inquisitively at everything, how to love deeply, without restraint or judgment or expectation. And that is how to be happy with what you have today, here, now. He does not expect me to live a certain way, or think a certain way, he only asks that I love him, with a soft touch and a soft voice, there in rain and shine, there by his side when it will be his time to let go of this earth.

As he sat down in the grass to ponder the miracle of a chew toy, I looked around me, at the weathered roofs, at the dust on my truck, streaked like tears from a recent, too brief shower. I looked at a church off in the distance, standing among the sparse gleam of headstones, an angel's marbled muse looking up to the sky with the soft knowing smile that is both grace and glory. There are no others around, just myself, my dog and my thoughts. I watched him play, there in those long summer moments, the constant mourning doves calling back and forth in time to a dog's tail, small things that remind us that we are so alive and so very lucky.

34

Lady and the Tramp Stamp

I've had some bad haircuts in my time, as with very fine but also curly hair, it happens. Barkley, however, has been spared getting shaved and groomed but for the occasional bath and nail trim.

Why is it a breed that *loves* the water and will cannon ball into any available pool or pond, hates getting baths? When he was a puppy he just got his baths in the tub. He wasn't too happy about it, but I could hold on to him and although I'd end up as wet as he was, we got it done.

When he was older, it didn't go so well. You know those wild-life clips from Africa that show the lion running and jumping on the zebra, taking it down in a flurry of legs and hair?

It was something like that.

So I had to take him to a "groomer." It was a lady recommended by his previous vet where we used to live, the groomer working from her home out in the country. I asked if she did larger dogs and she assured me she did all the time.

I left him. She was very friendly; the place spotlessly clean, her instruments shining and well cared for, the other dogs there, waiting to get picked up, looking content.

When I came back, she was there, with another girl I did not recognize. "I had to call for help," she said. Both of them were drenched, with wet hair, clothes, everything. There was water on the table, on the floor, several of their tools had been flung across the floor, and the picture on the wall was all askew. They looked like they'd been in a tornado and flood combined.

Barkley was in his pen drying out, with a scarf around his neck, looking ALL happy but not liking the scarf much.

"I'm *sooo* sorry." I said, "Please, let me pay you extra for your services."

As we left, she looked at me and said, "Miss, I appreciate the business, and hope you'll think of me if others ask about pet grooming. But *please* do not bring him back."

So baths got less frequent, but we managed. There were no more fashion accessories though, at least not until he came home with a square of fur missing from his lower spine.

It was some simple veterinary surgery to remove a small benign fatty growth from that area as well as four little skin tags on a couple of his legs. Common enough in older dogs but if he kept chewing on them it could do some harm, so off they came. At the same time, since he would be under anesthesia, his scheduled doggie dental cleaning and care was accomplished.

Barkley so loves Dr. H., and is oh-so-excited to get in the door and see her. I dropped him off in the early morning and could pick him up after I got off of work. He was not so happy with me when I picked him up.

He looked at me as if to say, "You told me some pretty girls were going to check my teeth and pet me, and I come home with Brazilian Bikini Butt."

Barkley is a "no fuss dog." Although he is AKC purebred and a hunting breed, he's lived a quiet life at home. It's been a simple life of water and dirt and running amok, not constant grooming and bows in his ears and dog couture. If I dressed him in costume as a food object or cute insect, he would likely steal the clippers and give me a Mohawk in my sleep.

He was neutered as a youngster; there's lots of good rescue dogs out there, so he wasn't going to reproduce, bloodlines or not, but he'd had a life of only routine fussing over, just enjoying being part of my family. His no-so-secret canine mission was that of most working dog breeds—to sniff every object in the entire world, peeing on anything that smelled even remotely like another male dog and then, having done so, trying to:

(a) eat it

(b) bark at it

(c) carry it around in his mouth

(d) hump it

But his teeth needed attention, so this had seemed like a good time to get it all done. The vet sent me home with some samples of dog treats that help with tartar, as well as a brush and some poultry flavored dog toothpaste (mmm, for breath that's barnyard fresh!) The veterinary technician said, "With a little practice your dog will enjoy his brushing."

I didn't tell her that the Storming of the Bastille was better received and less bloody than my attempt to apply a few drops of flea medication on his skin between his shoulder blades a couple of years ago.

I'd be *wearing* the chicken flavored toothpaste by the time we were through. I won't mention the look of disdain I'd get at a *pink* toothbrush. But the doctor only had his health in mind, and we talked about some alternatives to keep Barkley's teeth and gums healthy.

He did fine, though he whined a little when he did not get a full bowl of food the night before the procedure, by doctor's orders, and he was in a little discomfort when he came home. I had pain meds, but I could not give him one until the next morning, so he got much extra care and got to sleep with Mom on her bed, something normally not allowed.

I lay with him while he went to sleep, telling him he was still a handsome boy and even offering to show him the picture of me from the 80s when I had a mullet. He declined, it appeared, nodding off to sleep, happy that this day was done.

35
TSA Dog

Lying on the white carpeting was a small square packet, full of tiny holes, as Mom once again, looked through the phone book for a carpet cleaning service.

I'm not sure why the builder put in such light colored carpeting; perhaps they had no kids or pets, taking off their shoes before entering their Zen-like evening of peace and uninterrupted sleep.

They definitely didn't come home to trip over a half dozen dog toys, hoping that someone didn't leave a special gift in the corner, even with a friend or dog walker that comes over to let him out most days.

The day began with a squeaky toy that I named Robbie Roadkill, a flat little toy creature made out of stitched-together flat squares of cloth containing tiny squeakers, on which was only attached a plush little head and little legs. It was his new favorite thing, not just one squeaker to kill, but a *dozen.* It was also my new "do we have any bourbon left?" toy.

I had previously packed it in a suitcase while on a visit to friends out of town, so he'd have a toy and I forgot about it on my return. He was fascinated by the suitcase when he got his first glimpse inside one as a pup, once big enough to get up on the bed; but in the last few years, he'd shown no interest in it or its contents, as he was familiar with what it would contain.

After this last trip, Barkley started a vigil by the suitcase; I had no idea why, until now.

I'd had a very early wake up so when I got home from work, a nap was in order as soon as he had been fed and let out. I got out of my shoes and pants and shirt, put on some pajamas and lay down on the twin bed in the office, where a bit of sun had nicely warmed it.

It felt so good to be home. The trip to visit my friends was great, but I got called out of town immediately thereafter, a girlfriend staying with Barkley, the suitcase still with me.

This little bed, this little room, felt like shelter to me, warm, safe, nothing like being on the road for days on end. Nights in an unfamiliar hotel in another time zone, the air weighted with strange smells and the noise of the airport next door banging on your window like an unwanted peddler; and even if you stayed there willingly, you couldn't wait to get away. Where is the shelter in that, if only in the emptiness that reminds the heart of what it's capable of?

I told myself I could just go to sleep here and not wake up until morning.

Then I heard something.

"Squeak squeak squeak squeak squeak (ad nauseam)." Barkley had snooted open the canvas top of the suitcase in the master bedroom and grabbed Robbie Roadkill. I marched into the living room, took it away and tried to go back to my nap. I lay down. Ah. Silence. OK, now it's *much* too silent.

I walked back out into the living room. No Barkley. I looked down the hall, past the bathroom, into the master bedroom.

There in the darkened hall was this black apparition surrounded by a little cloud of something, looking like Pigpen in the Peanuts cartoon. He had something in his mouth and as he chomped on it, puffs of some type of a powder substance came out of it in little puffs, which then somehow combined molecularly with dog drool to make small gobs of dark sticky goop on the white carpeting. All *over* the carpeting.

"What in the world...?"

Chomp Chomp, Drool Chomp.

He'd got a package of powdered Chocolate Flavored Protein Drink out of my suitcase, figuring that after the squeaky toy was in there, the suitcase had transformed itself into some new and magical buffet. He did like to take things from other peoples suitcases for inspection, to the point where my friends Dorothy and MC referred to him as TSA Dog. "I'm sorry, Miss, but I will have to confiscate that pair of panties. They are more than three ounces."

But how did he get this one? The packet was inside a pocket *inside* the closed but not zippered suitcase. Don't ask me how he extricated that and *Dang it, that's my last pack!*

Chomp Chomp Drool

"Drop it Drop it! Outoutoutoutoutoutoutout!"

The package was full of holes, but it still contained some of its contents, most of the rest still unconsumed, by the looks of what was on the floor, smeared all around with dog spit and paws. I am thankful he hadn't tried to eat it, just play with it.

Then he started licking his paws. He got a taste of it now, and there was no going back.

Lick Lick Lick "No NO! Chocolate bad!"

I ran water in the big "Garden" tub, the only way I could think to get his paws clean quickly and at once, as he was determined to lick it all off. He does *not* like baths, but he needed to get in.

Note to self, putting peanut butter on one's fingers to lure the dog into a tub full of water with you is *not* a good idea, unless you're wearing Kevlar long johns, which Victoria's Secret does not stock.

LICK LICK "No, don't push!!! SPLASH!

BARK BARK BARK BARK

There would be no nap. There was now a stain that looked vaguely like Gorbachev's (or Fred Mertz's, I get them confused) birthmark in the hall ready for paper towels and cleaner. I now had a damp dog lying on the bed in the sun in the office, which only moments ago had an indentation of my tired head on the bedspread. I smelled like wet dog, peanut butter, and dog spit.

And I had this sudden hankering for chocolate.

36

Branch Manager

It was another weekend up at my Mr. B and MC's house in the northern part of the state. Whether it's in the home, at the Brew Pub, or at a local conservation club, there's just something wonderful about spending time with friends that know each other well. We know each other's quirks, faults, fears and history, so much to draw from, conversations, pets, family, books, and quips from movies. Conversations may be such that no one else understands what we are talking about, times when just certain words bring about unrestrained laughter.

This trip might be a little quieter though, and not just because EJ was out of the country and wouldn't be joining us. For at the age of fifteen, Schmoo, their black lab had passed away since my last visit, and I wondered how Barkley would process her physical absence even though her presence would always be in that house.

As I got dressed at home, Barkley saw the overnight bag and soon was pacing by the back door, trying to escape with me each time the door opened to carry something to the truck.

It does not matter that I have never abandoned him without friends in place for his care, or how many times I say, "I'll be back." He acts if he does not understand, as if his mind, though hearing words that he knows, forgets them or simply on receiving the words, finds no meaning in them until I actually return. Such it is with dogs: whether you are gone five minutes or five hours, they believe it was forever as you hope beyond reason that it will never be.

We made the drive in good time; Barkley started to get excited as soon as we exited the freeway toward their house. He knew the trip up here and a trip to EJ's house so well, he could almost sense when we were near the correct exit. Who knew what manner of play he'd experience this trip. He'd been to a very, very big pond otherwise known as a Great Lake, in which he got to paddle around on a long lead, parallel to the shore as we all walked. He'd napped with four cats, chased a squirrel and seen his first chipmunk.

But today looked like a good day for a long walk, back to the tree at the back of the property where, underneath, Schmoo now lay. We'd not had rain in a few days, the ground mostly dry, so when we arrived we let him off of his leash out in the back acreage. There was no way he could get into a road, and though a neighbor had a pond, there was no water on my friends' property.

We thought.

We'd forgotten about the big rain earlier in the week.

MC and I spotted the mud puddle after he did, Barkley running toward it at top speed as we cried "NOOOOooo!" moving in slow motion as if in some nightmare.

The term "puddle" was generous; it was mostly mud, into which he cannonballed with all the exuberance that a black lab can bring to any formula that contains H2O.

Splat!

He got out, and then jumped in again, as we caught up. There was no stopping him, and we just stood there laughing as he covered himself head to tail with mud.

Mr. B just stood there shaking his head saying, "He is *not* going to like the hose."

At this point, there was nothing we could do but lure him over to the neighbor's property line, look to see that there was no one around, and then release him though with an "oh, (ahem) NO, my, uh, dog is out! Please don't jump in the neighbor's pond!"

Splash! Into the clean pond he went, swimming around until he looked mostly clean so he could be called back to his own property, which he did, carrying a limb of a tree that weighed about as much as he did.

It only took a bit of time with the hose, and some serious wrestling moves, for Mr. B to get him clean enough to come into the house, something that both MC and I would have happily paid a cover charge to watch.

In the morning, it was time to go, and part of me remembered the last time we were here, when we said goodbye to Schmoo, knowing she would not be here on our next visit. In the trees, birds sang, believing in this moment that they are eternal, and at this moment I would like to believe they are. The sun looked down on us, creating shadows of the inextricable and incredible bond between friends, human and canine, there on the periphery of yet another year, another day, gone but always remaining.

The sun was warm on both fur and skin as we played with the dogs one last time, tramping our shadows into the grass, listening to the bark of birds of which the silver air was full.

Even though Schmoo is now gone, there were a lot of happy memories in this house, and more to be made.

37

On the Road Again

EJ and I had been together two years. My house purchase plans stayed a rental, part of me not willing to commit to buying a house yet, the rest of me always with him, visiting his home, that although wasn't mine, was home to me. But he was still living a fair distance away from where I lived and worked.

He always offered to come down to see me and sometimes, when tired, I said yes. But most weekends found Barkley and his favorite redhead shuttling back and forth like seasoned travelers, anxious to be with our other best friend, even if his seventy-year-old stove hated me, the plumbing had been through multiple Great Wars, and there were nights he worked quite late. In years to come, whatever the road brings, I'll recall these trips well. It was a time where I made my trek to shield and duty, and back again, to a small house that some might see as sometimes vacant, but I see as simply filled with warm presence, like held breath.

Tonight I got off work late, the news of a fatal accident on the freeway I take up north, delaying my travel. I went back to my place, played with Barkley, fed him, and called EJ, then hit the bed like some toppled Easter Island Statue, waking up, nose stuffy and stuffed into the pillow.

I opened my eyes, and Barkley was sitting by my bed, his Mr. Squeaky toy in his mouth, as much as saying, "get up already. Mr. S. and I are ready to go." It was morning already.

Barkley and I had a routine down. Now that I had two sets of dog beds and bowls, one for each place, rather than hauling them back and forth, I'd just buckle him in his harness after some exercise, and off we went, as early as we could get out, suitcase in tow.

Like most trips, I do not remember much of the drive, but my mind stays active, even as I paid attention to the road, thoughts rolled back like tide, exposing rocky shore.

I'd like to say the thoughts were anything of great wisdom, but they were only the disjointed musings of a mind not yet fully infused with caffeine, filtering the reports for work to be crafted, the words still jostling for position in my head. I thought of the local news, wondering if they cleaned up that bad accident I heard of last night. Then I wondered if someone crashed near that huge sign north of here that proclaims "*Hell is Real,*" reconciling my forgiving God with those words or the God that others say does not exist, because they can't explain Him in conventional scientific means.

With what I have seen in my life I'd have to side with the words of Henry Vaughan. He said, "There is in God a deep but dazzling darkness" so much that we won't understand for now, but which, if we look slowly, finds a place brimming with the potential of light.

Barkley, however, is having no such deep thoughts, making little doggie noises in the back seat that would translate to something like "ninety-nine boxes of treats on the wall, ninety-nine boxes of treats, take one down pass it around. . ."

I take that as a sign that I'd best concentrate on the road right now rather than sort out the nature of God, road signs, *or* the universe. Besides, up ahead we will stop, and he'll get a biscuit and I'll eat my peanut butter sandwich.

I know people that commute three or four hours a day. More people are living this way, not for their dream job but *any* job, given today's economy, only seeing their loved ones on the weekend. How different from those days of our parents' and grandparents' generation, where one lived in the same house forever, Dad driving fifteen minutes to work each day, days that are pretty much over. Our parents' definition of "distance" was a few simple miles, paved with unflagging faith that their life post-war would be prosperous and peaceful, populated with kind and familiar voices and faces. They would not have imagined the horns and traffic and strangers that use their middle finger as a turn signal.

Then, there are the people that, by the nature of their work, are on the road: truckers, military personnel, engineers, contractors, pilots. Such work sometimes requires hundreds of miles on the road or in the air each week, fueled by coffee and food best left in the cellophane.

But I've done it, gotten up at two o'clock in the morning for a mission that started at four o'clock. Getting up that early is just *not* natural; it's cold and oily dark, stubbing your toe on a wheel chock someone threw off to the side, as if there was a new Highland game of "Foreign Object Damage Toss." It's starting an engine that is not full of oil or gas but only cold personal contempt for your attempt to bring it to life when it clearly has a headache and wishes to be left alone. It's a long day, a cold bed, and a dinner that was intended to be eaten warm.

So, now, I don't mind a long drive, I don't even mind an airline flight. On those, I can read a book, or scribble some notes for my journal. If some guy in the next seat gets too flirty, a quick jot on my notepad in purposely large letters of "the striations on the distal end of the ulna indicate that the unsub attempted to saw the hands off" with a little smile usually gets him back to his in-flight magazine.

I preferred traveling with just Barkley by my side. We just drove. I didn't talk on the phone, fuss with my hair or my lip gloss, I paid attention to what was going on around me, the flash of a brake light up ahead, a reduction in visibility, the portent of storm clouds, indicating it was a good time to get off the freeway for a coffee and biscuit break. More than once we've gone through a drive-thru and ordered a hamburger with no condiments or bun. The voice from inside asks, "Oh, you're doing the low carb diet," and I respond, "No, but you'll see in a minute." He gets biscuits at the bank drive thru as well, barking as the little container with my check in it shoots up to the heavens, mysteriously reappearing with food.

When I speak of the drives, people from other states say, "But it's all flat, what is there to look at?" It is the scenery that my grandparents saw when they settled here, the sunny loneliness of vast tracts of earth that are outside of the limits of age and haste, where the fields and woods seem to hover in some inescapable equidistance that is both stasis and motion, fading as you near them, like mirages. It's not the beauty of the mountains, of the oceans, but it is beauty that lies with its beholding, like many things.

It's a commute, one that Barkley and I have been doing for a while now, and one that is a long monotonous continuation of undeviating road. It's a journey from dawn to dark and dark to daylight, through which I slowly slip around and ahead of those anonymous and deliberate vehicles that pass like shiny avatars. Even with the occasional 10-minute slow down by some trucker wishing to pass another trucker in the only open lane because he can go one mph faster, I make decent time.

I know he gets bored, so I will occasionally reach back, even as I look forward, giving him a pat or a treat. Some trips I take a small camera and with one hand, eyes forward, hold it up and take a picture of the back seat. I have no idea at the time what I've captured, but the results have been comical. One photo shows Barkley pulled to within five inches of the bag of cheese crackers on the armrest, a look on his face that was both intent and sheer frustration. Another photo shows him sticking his head up to the left of mine, sticking his tongue out at the camera, like a small child.

I wonder how much longer I'd be making this trip. EJ and I had casually floated the idea of marriage about, something serious under the surface of our talk, invisible in the depth of it. We loved each other, as friends for many years, then more. We've played with British car wiring and copper plumbing without ever arguing and he does not raise an eyebrow when I take off on an assignment for days or come home and set a potholder on fire trying to make dinner. Besides, more and more, he was becoming something that I thought only this furry backseat driver could be, that which I could not bear to be apart from for very long. Besides, Barkley loved him, as excited to see him each time as anyone I've known, recognizing in that man a soul who would never hurt either one of us.

A decision should probably be made to either go ahead and make that commitment, or just stay friends and take life a day at a time, living separate lives. In any case, I'm glad I have had this time with him, the support as we buried my Stepmom, the cancer not taking her, but pneumonia after battling Alzheimer's for too long. Then a diagnosis of cancer in Big Bro earlier this year, late stage Esophageal, worry that I wear on me, like a clock.

For now, if only just now, I will not worry, I will watch the scenery. I also watch the other cars and how they are being driven, adjusting my distance from them accordingly. There are the cars that just plod along, ten mph less than the speed limit in the fast lane, blinders on, moving forward with all the speed of a mule in that steady and unflagging hypnosis of the unaware. There's the "go speedy racer go" vehicles that zip in and out without looking, without signaling, the marks of their previous battles upon their scarred fenders. However, the mule is often more dangerous than Speedy racer.

We've developed a system of driving, Barkley and I. He doesn't suddenly bark "Look, a squirrel!" when I'm trying to pass a truck at seventy mph, and I don't get out of shape about the other drivers and startle Barkley from a nap with a loud "Did you see that moron?" Gauge but don't engage. I watch and I think as the miles fall behind.

For years, I just moved as fast I as could, traveling so as to leave grief behind, lots of photos of planes and places, lots of possessions but nothing that truly felt mine, no square ground of the earth really home, no person other than my immediate family, let too close. I chose that, was fully aware of it, and I carried that knowledge with me like a flag, a quality as lonely as it was proud.

Then Barkley showed up in my life, a conscious decision to bond with something, to take a risk on flesh and bone that I knew too well, is so very fragile. I was realizing, as he and I found our way through more than one move, that a home was not some plot of earth or address. Seeing myself through the eyes of another so very much like me, I realized that a home was someplace within, the last place I had thought of looking for it.

I think about that, pulling into the drive between tall trees, a light on in the window, in anticipation of my arrival. Barkley is pulling on his harness that tucks him safely into the back seat, now that we have not just arrived, but that we are home.

38
Simple Evening

It was supposed to be a simple evening. EJ had been overseas for a couple of weeks on business and was flying in to see me for a quiet evening. We enjoyed the evenings like this, making dinner together, both of us loving to cook. Then we'd play an old fashioned board game or take Barkley for a long walk. EJ would play with him, talking to him as if he were human, while I got a bubble bath. Then we'd curl up on the couch, Barkley usually shoving his way between us, to lounge against us until everyone was sleepy. Weekends we'd play with the tools in either his garage or mine, building on things stronger than wood.

Somewhere over the course of a friendship of many years and a bonding over bad knees and bad dogs, EJ became a big part of my life. I'd missed him a lot while he was gone, our talks of the future becoming more serious. Tonight, I was wondering, would he pop the question?

But first, I had to feed Barkley and take him outside to potty.

My neighborhood is a quiet one, with both young and retired couples. I've a police officer on one side of me, a young couple on the other. All of them are great neighbors. The young couple has a rescue dog, a smaller yellow lab/terrier mix. Barkley likes to bark at him out the front window, but is mostly ignored, despite his attempts at engaging the hound by leaving his calling card on the front bushes.

The block was quiet, so in a hurry to get ready, I let Barkley out to do his business. After that, he sniffed everything, then trotted in through the garage and went into the house, off leash, just as he'd done several hundred times. He'd patiently wait in the kitchen for his treat, while I cleaned up the deposit and a few others made earlier in my yard in the dark. One thing about a ninety pound dog, if the barking does not scare burglars away, the land mines in the yard might. As based on volume, they might think you have a grizzly bear on premises. So I kept one of those big long-handled scoopers that is open on one end and has a secondary shovel-like thing to help gather everything up.

But as I finished that up, lo and behold, the neighbor arrived home with baby and dog in tow, the dog jumping out of the car off leash to go into his house.

I wasn't sure I could get all of his landmines in the scooper in one trip, but with careful balance, I did. It really was the perfect plan. Until Barkley heard the dog from deep within the house and rushed out the back door, out the open garage door, racing over to the neighbor's drive to finally meet their dog.

I rushed over to collect him, wielding a pooper scooper that had more crap in it than most political campaign commercials. Barkley was over in the dog's face with the typical Labrador retriever "hi there hi there hi there, play with me play with me play with me" like some demented door-to-door salesman.

The neighbor dog did *not* like Barkley in his space, trying to make friends on his turf, and immediately launched into "bark bark bark bark" complete with crazed eyes and snapping teeth inches from Barkley's face.

It was all show; the teeth were not making contact though they could have, but Barkley was freaking out, never having been set upon by a weird stranger (if he'd on-line dated as the rest of us have, it might not have been so traumatic). So I lunged for his collar as my neighbor pulled his dog away, one arm stretched out, the other swinging up, not realizing what I had in my other hand (yes, you can see this one coming).

Pooper Scoopers make a dandy catapult with the right angle and force.

The load of dog poop went *up*, and then, as gravity is likely to make it do, it came *down.*

Splat! Splat! Splat! Splat! Splat!

It was raining down on their driveway like a bad day in Beirut (so glad my coat is brown).

The dogs are now suddenly friends, sniffing and wagging tails, the neighbor apologizing profusely as he takes his dog and the baby from the car seat and goes inside to get the family situated.

Barkley back inside with the door firmly closed, I got paper towels, a plastic bag, a broom and water to clean their driveway, which I was doing, hair disheveled, looking like I was a very sore loser in a game of Poop Paintball.

Just then EJ rolled up, all dressed up, more than for typical travel, with a bottle of expensive wine.

I think about all he could have said if he weren't laughing so hard, but what he said was, "Would you like red or white wine with that?"

39

Field and Dreams

It's the hour when the sun is high and your heels are blistered. The sky is cold, the trees providing no shelter as you continue to walk and search the horizon. Your legs ache and your vision is focusing, not on the task at hand, but on some hoped-for mirage in which the chair and a cold beer will magically appear. You're tired and cold, wishing only for the heat of a small fire to warm you from the inside out.

But someone else wants to go on. Those big brown eyes that look up at you are saying that it's pheasant season and they are not done hunting yet.

Actually, Barkley was not a hunting dog, he was just tagging along. His hunting skills are limited to socks and stray underwear. With the many visits out to check on my Dad to ensure his well-being, vacations for bird hunts and other outdoor adventures had to be put aside. But today we were out with friends on a huge stretch of private land, as they hunted a few game birds for the freezer. He minds enough to keep back with me and not get in the way. Still, I hoped Barkley would pick up some pointers here, but the only pointer he tried to pick up was a little female who quickly rebuffed his interest.

We watched those dogs skirt and track, making J hook maneuvers that would make a fighter pilot proud even if he were a beginner. Barkley though, did do the occasional point, if only on a twig. Yes. Point. He did it first at about six months of age, pointing at a Baby Ruth wrapper on the ground. Then it was a ball cap dropped by someone, then a pigeon. I called the lady I got him from. She said, "Labrador retrievers don't point, that's just a puppy thing." Tell that to Barkley. He points at birds, bacon and if company is over, to that pair of underwear I accidentally dropped on the floor while putting laundry away.

Today, we were mostly out for a hike and the company of friends, the birds today being secondary. "What do you think, Barkley? A couple more miles?" He looked as if he genuinely understands my intent until there is that sound, the tiny whoosh of air being displaced by winged creatures with a brain the size of a pea and a breast that calls out for succor or bacon. Birds! Dogs! More Birds! Woof Woof Woof! "No Barkley, you're scaring off all of the birds, come back here!!"

My friends took it in good stride; this was just an outing, not a serious hunt. We'd walked for what seemed like ten miles, while the others fanned out up ahead with their dogs, leaving us junior birdmen to trail behind, watching for brass, looking out for wake turbulence. It's nice, being just a tiny group, the single monotony of our goal, striding forward, chests heaving, moving fast, the world suddenly coming to a stop with a small sign from a retriever.

It's that glorious moment in time where the motion of a wasted world of daily activities, of cell phones, meetings, and doing chores, comes down to that one moment of freedom and decision. That moment when the world accelerates and then just suddenly stops, there on the precipice, there in that space between a retriever, hunter and bird. A moment in a hunter's life, that evocative quality of living, in which the forward motion toward the game stops, but then loops back, toward you. A loop that completes the circle of predator and prey, waiting only for the curl of a dog's body, the curl of your finger, to close that circuit, and release it all with one sharp sound that breaks the line of containment.

Barkley is learning, and he for once, stood at attention when a bird was sensed, almost motionlessly, only the subtle tremble in his eyes, the despair of ever being released from the hold that's been placed on him, a responsibility he picked up willingly, if only for you. Yet, as much as he's trying, he might run on back to you, caught up at the moment, trying to please, it's a learning curve for both of you, but that free and loving heart is heavenly to see.

We may not get a bird today for our dinner table; Barkley is not trained for this, but we forgive each other, even as we make mistakes and learn. It is a bond between him and me. For me, it is not a substitute for something lacking in my life, but an outlet for the warmth I harbor in my soul, seeking a place for the waters of my emotion to go when all else is damned up.

He's my confidant; he's my fashion critic (jeans and t-shirt again? Well, if you insist), he's a soft-hearted Kleenex if I cry.

He's given me renewed hope in the capacity of the heart, as his ability to love is boundless. He'll stay on alert, face aching with a grimacing growl, keeping predators at bay while I'm at work. He's been the soft nuzzle of concern on my neck after a coughing fit during a bad winter cold, and he welcomes the friends that I shoot with into the house while keeping those that wish to harm at bay.

Now, he was getting older, grey abundantly showing up in that black hair. Yet still, when woken by my soft snore from the office bed he'll move away from the heater, to my side as swift, as strong as ever, even as he slows. He looks at me with brown eyes more humorous and honest than anyone I know, soft paw on my arm, content simply to be by my side because I'm there. Like the rest of my friends, his needs are simple, his demands of me only warmth, faithfulness and time to go out and play.

He's taught me that money doesn't matter; he's as happy with a stick as an expensive toy; satisfied with a sleeping bag in a tent with me more than a luxurious pillow top mattress. Life is simple; someone to love and something cold to drink, well loved toys to play with and a safe place to sleep.

I know he will love the life that awaits us, one with less loneliness and more adventures, going where we go, with an open heart and a bigger family. For today, I think I will just give my four-legged best friend a little more time outdoors, maybe a bird for dinner if we're lucky. That's all we need, some open sky and something in the distance to seek, a bird or perhaps a dream. Perhaps, that's all any of us really need.

I give him one last little pat as we get up and move out toward a fading sun. His muscles rippling like silk under my hands, yet more precious than anything man-made. He races ahead, legs leaving the ground all at once, an outstretched leap toward his future, as if he has lost contact with the earth.

40

View From a Porch

It was that time of the evening when things grow both restless and weary. The sun had dipped below the horizon, just enough light remaining to make out the forms of a couple of bicycles strewn across a lawn down the road, abandoned by children called in to supper.

Their house was dark but for the faint glow from the front window, the activity and the movement all in the back of the house, where the kitchens were typically found. The children had no doubt that the bikes would still be there in the morning, not yet versed in the duplicity of some humans, those raised to simply take without effort that which they have not earned.

Let them enjoy this idyllic time, the days of doubts and of cold, dark nights would come soon enough.

For me, the thoughts were anything but dark. EJ had proposed, and Barkley agreed that "yes" was the best response. This place that had been a visited place for me would soon be my home.

I loved the neighborhood. It is an older area, some of the houses a hundred years old, many of the families composed of the children and grandchildren of immigrants from Central Europe and Ireland. The homes are small, meticulously maintained, most with porches. There are no burglar alarm signs, no bars on the doors. The Catholic Church, which many of the families in the neighborhood belong to, is within an easy walk. Most of the houses have porches with more than one American flag that hangs from them, proud symbols of a nation born into or adopted as one's own. There are an equal number of yard gnomes and Virgin Mary statues, both often bearing the same swatches of fresh color.

The houses themselves are grey, white, brown or brick, no trendy Victorian doll house colors, no urban renewal shades of yuppie reclamation. The houses and porches are the shades of time and shadow and quiet murmured voices gathered between columns, as if time and breath had made them all one quiet color, a hushed vestibule where all is forgiven.

In my grandparent's day, families would escape the heat of the home and the kitchen when summer came, breathless and sultry. Children played quietly on the wooden steps while adults sipped on tea and shared the stories of their city, their world, the words of their experience and not simply what was reached across an anonymous screen. Young adults courted, fell in love, and started their own lives, their own families, on other porches, likely not more than a few miles away. There was sameness to it, a safe continuity, an opening with each other and their world.

So it is, I often sat out on my porch with Barkley in the evening, sometimes with a friend, sometimes alone, sipping a drink, waving at a neighbor walking by but usually the only one out here, watching the clouds assassinate the stars, until it was cold enough I had to go in.

My Dad had such a porch in their first house, one that looked upon a wide open world. He also has a large baseball bat by the front door, his shotgun given to a family member when he was no longer able to handle it safely with his age. But he is ready to defend his home; however he can, if the world turned on its ear. Open does not mean naive, and the bonding of family in such places, also increases the will to protect. It took him a Great War and the loss of a wife and a baby to fully realize the taste and savor of peace and he was not going to give it up easily. He is the gentlest of men, but I know he would have defended his family against evil had it been necessary.

I thought about Dad this night as I sat on this porch with Barkley waiting for EJ to get home. I grew up where you did not have to lock your doors unless it was zucchini season, and some zucchini gardener tagged your front seat with a bag of the overabundant veggie. But given the nature of my life, I was more than aware of what darkness waited at the edge of town.

Perhaps I should have been worried about being alone out here, armed with just a big dog that in a burglary likely would be thinking, "Hey look at the great bone this guy in a mask gave me." Labs aren't known as guard dogs, but that's not why I got him.

It was almost dark, the sound of a neighbor's mower from a distance, silenced as the sun bit into the crust of the earth. Barkley was attached to a line that connects a point on his harness above his shoulder to the porch, a way for me to get him up and out and in, after I blew out my knee--now simply a way to ensure that he can't get out into the street should squirrel attempt warfare while we're sitting out here.

He didn't fuss much, just content to watch, quietly looking at his world head on. Then there was a rush of movement at ten o'clock moving to two o'clock He shot off the porch, and down the long steps, barking in a manner I'd only heard him bark once or twice in my life, teeth showing, barking at the heels of a young man in dark pants and hoodie, running past.

It was not running as in "I'm late and I'm going to get grounded" or "I am going to try out for track" but the fleeting steps of one wishing to be gone before detection in an area he didn't live in, gravel flying from beneath his fleeing feet.

Barkley, who suffers joggers, skateboards, the neighbor with the annoying remote controlled car and kids of all ages and sizes on bikes whizzing up and down his sidewalk, nearly nailed this guy. I watched as he ran even faster past those teeth, as ninety pounds of muscle and bark came out of the dark at him, determined to keep that motion of ill intent away from his Mom.

The line ran out, the bungee portion of it keeping the stop from being painful, just abrupt, and that young man kept running.

Minutes later a cop car cruised past. Someone had tried to steal something from a car but ran away, it was said.

I'd not been in any danger; the kid had just been trying to get out of the neighborhood, and though I went back inside, it was not to hide, but to give Barkley a treat. His action surprised me a little. Was it instinctive or did he perceive an intent not visible by simple motion? I looked at him and he cocked his head at me with a goofy Lab expression, and the image of him teeth bared, and hair on fire seemed like a different creature.

But perhaps he too, has within him the trait that my Dad does, amidst the peaceful nature, the honor to protect and a love of family as sincere as his own unfeigned and honest soul. Both of those meant to him what God means to a believer and if I were threatened he would not hesitate to pick up his truth and ready his sights.

Cities sprawl out to the suburbs, which sprawl out to small towns and villages, bringing with them crime and change. Nothing remains the same, and wishing for the past often means just wishing for the best parts of it, which isn't always the reality of it. But I have no regrets for choosing this simple life near the city with a big black dog, and soon a husband, a life I'd not trade for any fancy suburban home. I have no regrets for the life I'm going to embark on. I'd rather live simply and true to my heart, looking at the world head on, not hiding from the truth or the world, simply standing firm on a hundred-year-old porch, next to the shadow of my furry black guardian.

41

A Wedding

The house was decorated for the reception, a few friends and family gathered. The dining room held a cake that had on it, not a bride and groom, but a time traveling machine known as the Tardis and a Dr. Who and Amy figure from the BBC Sci -Fi series, Dr. Who. It is a non-conventional cake topper for a family that will be anything but conventional.

I missed having Barkley here, but the combination of "look! people!" black dog hair and white dresses, and a table full of "treats!" was a viral YouTube video waiting to happen, one I did *not* want to see. But we were only going to spend our wedding night at a romantic Bed and Breakfast. Then we would swing by the Doggie Day Camp, where Barkley would remain tonight and pick up the rest of our family, for what's a honeymoon without a little dog hair.

One in my bridal party is in a kilt, and I smile, this being a day of many surprises. I am in a Renaissance style wedding dress, MC is Maid Marion of Honor and Mr. B is the best man. The minister is a personal friend, a retired pastor and author, someone who understands words and emotions and hearts, marrying for himself for the first time in his fifties to a young lady, a pilot friend of mine, in her thirties.

There is no one else we'd rather have marry us.

Our wedding. It was not just a day; it was a decision, one we made together. We could embark on this journey, one that any statistic will tell you is a risk, or we could stay safe, keeping hearts in check, telling ourselves it's probably for the best.

If I had thought that, ten years ago, I would not be wondering about the best way to get dog hair off a wedding gown. I wouldn't be here, so very happy.

We wake to the earth's silent ticking, chasing the time that is still unaccounted for, rushing headlong from nights of God's silence to days of great discovery. We can stay in, intact for one slow, sure, unremarkable day, gathering useless possessions and people around us, as what sparked our dream fades to an almost sleeping ember. For many people, that is their safety. We can just sit and talk about it, the changes we need to make, the things we wish we could do, but talk is just that, talk - arming ourselves with the satisfaction of courage without the inconvenience of risk. Or we can cast off our fear, gather those things around us that are precious, shedding that which only seeks to hinder us and head out into the world, eyes wide open.

What is ahead is unknown, often coming at us, so towering and fast, one can sense from it neither distance nor time. You can treat it with fear, no different than standing on the edge of a cliff, dreading that feeling as the ground falls away, the tiny rocks clamoring down like the first throw of dirt on a pine box. Or you can treat it as a perceived feast, as a wafer on the tongue, a leap of faith into that place that is devoid of time and regret, while that which held you back runs somewhere far afield, away from soundless guns.

I know where my home is, and it's not four walls. I know who my friends are and they could care less about the things I own, where I live, or how old I am. As I look at my husband, at a photo of a big black dog in a frame, I know I have the comfort of a life in which, if only for a moment, I meant the absolute world to someone. That is something you can never buy, like the heat of steady flame that warms you from the inside out.

As the vows echoed in a room full of happy toasts, stories were told of Barkley, how he brought all of us together, of those he has healed and bonded. For we are his pack, as we are each others, love being, not a journey, but something that gently brings us back home.

42

Life's Artifacts

On the desk is a shell, unearthed from the sand on a distant ocean as a child, the spiral whorl of the shell drawing in my gaze, inviting me in deeper. On the shelf overhead, a handful of tiny rocks rest on polished wood, all pretty much the same size, yet so different. One is clearly a piece of fossilized shell, expected on an ocean's edge perhaps, but not on a Great Lake. Another has holes in it, like Swiss cheese from the power of the water. All but the large shell are from a stretch of shore not far from home, on which one evening several years ago, three friends walked with two black labs, the male following protectively behind the female, both just happy for the company.

Mr. B's black lab Schmoo had made that trip many times, I'm sure. But that day was a first for Barkley. I could almost hear the thoughts in his head as he looked at it with a "that's the biggest pond I had ever seen" look on his face.

Animals weren't allowed loose on the beach, so with a long leash, Barkley simply bounded in, swimming parallel to the shore as we walked. Schmoo, too old to swim, but not to dream, carefully walked in hard sand with those she loved, memories of happy times with her people here, splashing across her face.

Finally, Schmoo sat, Barkley emerged from the water, and as the sun set, I waved off to the West. There, a big city rose like Oz, a city where unknown to me on that day, someone who loved me quietly waited.

Outside the window, a plant opens up, spilling forth its seed onto the soil. I remember days of working in the flowerbeds that my Mom so lovingly maintained. After her death, I kept it going as long as I could for my Dad, until adulthood called me away. As I toiled in the garden, the sun kissed the top of my head, the touch a benediction, a blessing.

I had not yet learned of other kisses, the ones in the crook of the neck where the head joins the body and the body knows not its limitations. The one that dances on the skin like light that falls upon it, outstretched hands gathering fistfuls of flowers imprinted upon starched cotton. I had not yet learned that love is not just as wild as the flowers; it's as fragile and elusive as glass; that in nature, the most delicate of things are often trod underfoot as they go unnoticed.

At the bookstore recently, an engineering manual, two generations old, was opened to browse. In it was an ancient leaf, carefully pressed within the pages, the person who had done so likely long gone. I have many books like that old book, purchased from stores that contain more light than dust, yet containing within them things old and forgotten, things that in the wrong hands would only grow older. Finding the right one is like finding treasure, fingers tracing the spine, fingers that are gentle and forgiving, not wishing any further scar upon that which binds.

Such books find their way home, where they lay looking out from under leaded glass, pulled out to be read on late nights, the mind marveling that other minds marveled, the mysteries, the mistakes, playing out across the pages as if they were penned today. They tell their tales like the lonely, animated elderly, to anyone who is willing to listen, lessons given without rancor or heat, so many words that need to be said while they can still be heard.

On the top of the bookshelves are blown glass bowls, inviting someone to fill them with something, but remaining more beautiful in their solitude. They are containers, yet they are as much contained by the air around them, being nonetheless beautiful for the empty space they shape and form.

The bowls lie in the shadow of a photo. The frame captures a giant of a man and a younger woman, appearing dainty in his shadow though she's taller and sturdier than many men. They are clad in black leather, the form of a motorcycle in front of them. The sun shines on hair the color of copper, on shared features that confirm their familial bond and their heritage, yet the thickness of the leather hints at the outside temperature.

They brought to that day the smell of the wind, drawing it in as it wound up through mountain passes, exhaling it on that rush that is horsepower and gravity as they descended back down into the valley like flying fish before the prow of a ship. They look as if they've ridden two hundred miles, but by their smiles, they look as if they could ride forever.

As I look at it, I'm aware of my own heart beating within this vessel which has traveled so many miles, will travel so many more. I pick up the phone to call him, that man I call Big Bro, the voice tired, but happy to hear from me, the words filling empty air. Like me, he is aware of the fragility of the body, the heart, the lines of blood coming in, blue and needing oxygen, the red lines flowing back out, the heart, like a busy road's roundabout, the movement and flow of blood keeping him alive. The heart beats along with the whoosh of the machinery that monitors him now, but he only laughs.

I don't know how he does it, staring down into the whorl of something as old as time, something that is always waiting. How much easier to pretend it doesn't exist? How much easier to raise a fist and curse Him who created a body as fragile as it is strong, so many different ways it can be broken and bruised, some beyond fixing. But the laughter is recognition, that even as we all will die, today we live, for where there is living blood and water, there is joy. Our hands reach out, not to each other, separated by a thousand miles, but to themselves, clasped in buoyant not bitter prayer.

We talk of those days along the shores of the water, the floors of the forest, the things we unearthed, rocks and sticks and shells, and even occasional bone and brass. Some of those things found their way home, others were left where they lay, left as future treasure.

I loved him as a child, as I do now, because he never made me automatically play the field nurse when we all played soldier, for showing up at the playground to keep the schoolyard bullies away. I love him because he is gentle in his size, yet knowing, had I said the word, he would have thumped the one that long ago broke my heart, even as he understood why I would never ask that of him.

I've seen him laugh so hard that he cried tears that would not come otherwise. I've seen his face turn to stone, there where the seas fell, and men drown. I love him because he never cared for convention even as his life is one of structured order and solitude, even as he is one of many that together forge service and honor.

I still recall the day as a teen, when I did a long cross country to build flight time, and landed near the Naval base where he was stationed. Getting a crew car from the FBO, I got directions onto the base and to his place. But how was I to find his home among hundreds of battleship gray dwellings, all of the same shape and form, bearing within, seemingly identical lives? He gave me the general street directions and simply said, "You'll know it when you see it." I did, the big "FOR SALE BY OWNER" sign with the giant pink flamingo sticking out of the yard, visible a hundred yards away.

Everyone asks how he is doing now, but he discusses little of his cancer treatment, makes no complaints, offering neither prediction nor guess, and I understand why. His future to me is unknown, but he is a constant and prefers to live each day as if it is constant, even as we are both aware it is indeed so transient. So we tell our tales, especially those as we ran as children along the edge of the waters, along the rim of the earth as though we and we alone were its inhabitants and guardians.

The picture with the motorcycle stands over other shelves of glass and bone and rock, many of them, capable of smashing the others, yet all a part of something big, something that is more than memory. There among them, two pieces of paper, on which lie two names, marking not just a seating arrangement at a wedding reception, but a moment in time. I hold one of them up to my nose and breathe in the scent of the paper, of cold air and a warm kiss, there along the nape of my neck, as gentle as the sun, as protective as armor and I smile.

There are so many things on those shelves that most would not notice: small artifacts, strewn across the wood, pieces of time and place, of breath suspended, and words not necessary for us to hear. There are pieces of the past, portents of the future, the tears and the shouts, the still and the peace, the power to be afraid, the freedom to live anyway.

Then I open up another book, a newer book among many, of warriors and maidens, of fairy tales and spaceships. Within it lies a dried red rose, saved for something I cannot articulate, kept in the throes of that hurt that even the most intelligent believe can be forgotten if it is hidden. I take it out, carefully brushing the pages as I do, so that no remnant remains, not even dust, as I carry that long, fractured goodbye out to the trash.

I step out of the house to new beginnings, down the steps that lead into the spruce trees, the trail past the garage just a thin scar upon the earth. My feet step on bits of branches scattered about. A cone from a tree shatters under my foot, bearing fragments down into dried needles and tufts of rabbit fur, deep into the soil, bringing its richness to the heart of the earth.

43

Getting to Home

I remember a phone call the first time my friend, Tam, house- and dog-sat for me when I had business that kept me away from home for a few days.

"Is everything OK?" I asked, aware that there was a forecast of severe weather that night.

She said - "I didn't know Barkley was afraid of thunder."

I replied, "He isn't!'

She said, "Well, as soon as it started he climbed into bed with me and is plastered to my side."

I laughed. "That's not fear, that's just an excuse to sleep with you, and he figured you wouldn't be onto him."

I hated being away from Barkley. Only married a couple of months, I also hated being away from my husband, who was away on a business trip. I ran a quick calculation, and realized

I've spent over ten years of my life sleeping in a hotel room (or tent, vehicle, or the back of a plane). I wouldn't have gotten Barkley had I still had that schedule. But the last few years, I've been home a lot more, in a position that directs others doing most of the work away from home. Though intellectually I miss full time field work, I would rather be home, even if my four-legged roommate occasionally chases rabbits in his sleep and snores.

One thing I didn't miss and that was jet lag. The jet lag is more than a myth; it's a sledgehammer of weariness that hits you as soon as the aircraft door opens up, no matter what time it is. You're lucky if you get a long layover, where you have a few hours to wander ancient streets, the mazes of alleyways and churchyards and cemeteries of a small village, breathing in air that is laden with wood smoke and history. You're lucky if you have time to finally nap on long hot afternoons; sheets wrapped around you like a scratchy shroud, pretending you are home in your own bed instead of under a wall on which hang pictures of landscapes erased a hundred years ago.

There is the night after night of sameness. The bed looks like any bed in any hotel. Dinner is canned soup heated in the microwave, not because there is no room service or restaurant, but because you've had all the interaction with the world you can stand for the day, and you just want something hot to eat all alone. The mini bar beckons, but you don't go there either, not for the tiny little mortgage you pay with each clink of the little bottle that will only briefly relax your sapless limbs. The room is quiet, but in your head are the words of those that cannot be stilled, the ones that called you here, to this city, this week, where what little sleep you get will only be when the sodden match that is your brain, has nothing left with which it can spark.

There are the mornings you wake, not knowing what time it is, or what country you are in, and for a moment you pause in your hotel room, breathing heavy with fear as you orient yourself to your surroundings. You look outside, not knowing what you will see, having arrived in total darkness. A lovely village full of sight and sound and cobbled steps, or the war ravaged industrial town, a visage of smoke and ash, gaunt staring rubble rising out from sand, dirt and weed with an air of profound desolation that needs no further words.

It was a life of constant motion and travel, phone calls and emails home or abroad from loved ones living the same life, including that one in which you are told "I can't do this anymore," as you sit helpless and shaking 2000 miles away. You don't argue; your only response as the proverbial dial tone growls in your ear is the flinging of a shoe that strikes the wall with a single, shattering blow. The remaining nights you simply sat, as if listening to something very far away or so close as to be contained within you. The phone lay silent, but you did not. You called someone you trust, who also lives on the road and has been through this, to let it out, and then go on living. Certain types of lives demand sacrifices, but you can no more change that, than you can change what is essential for you. You continued with your duty, for it and order were the only constant that you know.

It's simply part of who we were, traveling where our skills were needed, not because your friends and family meant any less, but because responsibility carries with it its own honor. It was a life of many hotels, and meals probably best eaten in low light. It was memories, transparent and weightless, that scattered around us like leaves, blown without destination by winds that forever change.

But tonight the sounds of my own house are all around; the wind in the eaves, the soft breathing of a dog, and the tap of a branch against the porch railing. From within the walls, comes the rumble of heat; the house sighs, as do I.

Barkley makes that little sound that lets me know he is dreaming, good dreams I hope, his legs twitching as he runs after invisible rabbits.

There is comfort in such sounds, the creaks, the murmurs, whispers of earth and sky and people, quiet tears in a hotel room or laughter, sounds evocative of life and death and struggle, things we've been aware of all our lives but never really understood until now. Sounds and words like faded letters on a road sign, not pointing us to where we need to be, but letting us know we were on the right path.

Barkley wakes with a start, and comes on over, giving me that look that he wants up on the bed, where he is not allowed.

"OK, just this once," a phrase he has heard so many times, his plea and my argument and defeat a ritual, that simply makes us smile. He jumps up on the blanket that's folded on top of the bedspread, to protect it, does a 360 degree turn and lies down. On nights my husband is home, Barkley simply goes to his dog bed, there alongside of us, conceding to him who is the final protector, a pat and a treat his reward for concession.

There is no room service, there is no big TV, there are journals and books and more books, tools left about mid-function as a mind takes yet another bend in solving the puzzle of the day. There is dog hair and dust and an old refrigerator that operates on sheer will. There is a stained glass window, as old as I, that replaced what was once a mundane view of a yard, a window alive with colors that glow, when all color everywhere has failed the sky.

For no matter how dark things have been, there will always be that light that awaits you, nipping with sharp but gentle teeth at the shadows. It is home, and there is nowhere I'd rather be.

44

What Price Love?

What Price Love? Today all told - $811.46. That's in addition to the $329.04 twelve days ago.

All to a tiny, pretty blond woman in a white lab coat named Alice who talked to Barkley down on her knees, at his level, looking into his eyes, like he was a human. I swear he talked back to her.

It was another trip to the vet. The soreness and slight limping that showed up a couple of months after the wedding, first thought to be muscle strain or early arthritis did not respond to the drugs for that, even after a couple of weeks of very limited activity. Over only a couple of days, a slight limp went to full limp. Last night he refused food and wouldn't put his foot down, hopping on three legs. I was back at my old home, still commuting as my job was there, at least for now. This morning, while squatting to potty in the yard, he fell over, like cow tipping, without the moo. He was able to get up and slowly hop into the house with an "I meant to do that!" but with too much effort. Dr. H. was called and then work, as I would not be going in until later.

We were there by ten o'clock for the x-rays we'd discussed earlier. Don't ask me how I got him into the truck since he can't jump, but being part Valkyrie really comes in handy.

The images on the x-rays were such that a radiology specialist was consulted to look at the possibility we both were aware of, but weren't going to say yet: Appendicular osteosarcoma, a very aggressive bone cancer that manifests itself at the onset in lameness, the owner often trying other treatments until it's already spread to the lungs. My family has had large dogs before, so I know that lameness in a large-breed dog that does not promptly resolve with symptomatic therapy is a red flag we must check out. So here we were, waiting, the silent ticking of his life in my ear. I wished EJ were here, but he was many miles away on a business trip.

While the images went to the radiologist, I went back to work, if only to the office, hiding in the coat closet once to cry so no one would see. When you're like the TV character known as "Gibbs," you can't get caught crying.

Dr. H. called me with a sound in her voice that reflected some hope. There was no visible tumor on this first set of x-rays and the specialist said the bone didn't have that "Swiss cheese look" you don't want to see. It does not mean that cancer wasn't there, just not having manifested itself yet on x-ray. But it gives us time to look at other things, minor infection, simple inflammation; he's faking it to get more treats...

I could have brought him home, but with a huge winter storm approaching the next day that might strand us for days, it was agreed they would keep him with their other boarded dogs to monitor and run some more tests. This would also help in keeping him quiet for a few days while I went up north to home for a night or two, a trip in the truck he would not want to make in pain, time to build a ramp so he can go out in the backyard without even those few stairs. I brought his bed to which I added layers of foam underneath between the bedding and cover to keep him off the floor that could be cold, and added his toy and his treats

I imagine I'll be writing a couple more checks later. I don't mind. We do a lot for love: we learn, we grow, we take chances, and we hurt.

Most of us have lost someone close to us in our lives. A parent, a spouse, a friend, a beloved pet. It does not matter what form love takes, it becomes part of us, and losing it is like losing part of our very selves, leaving phantom pain that bites with sharp teeth. We all know that every life must end, but when it ends much too young or abruptly, it is just so hard to accept. For the true sublime blindness of love is its willful hesitance to fully embrace the mortality of all we hold dear.

I remember a moment at Dad's place not long ago, walking inside, and seeing my Dad so still in his chair, it appeared he wasn't breathing. For just an instant, everything went into high definition, the warmth of the room, the sun glinting off my old piano against the wall, Dad's glasses on the table. In the brief, terrible night that existed when I closed my eyes and then opened them again to see him smiling, I got a glimpse of the grief that waits for all men, which made the light around me now, so very, very vivid.

I am not alone in this perception. Think of the ancient paintings you have seen in a museum. Look at that life force that exists in those faces, in the bloom of color in a rosy cheek, the glint of light on a warrior's steel or the whispered movement of clothing as a woman lies upon a velvet cushion. All belie the fact that the persons in these visages are now only framed by the earth. For that moment, in those paintings, they are still so alive, the canvas containing more than their form, but their breath, something the artist understood all too well.

I look at pictures of myself and of the daughter I gave up for adoption and only met as an adult, wondering if decades from now, the upcoming generations of our women will remember the strength and love from which they were born. I look at words I penned even five years ago, words that don't exist now in the same world, even though they were placed in space with these same hands on this old computer, as the same old clock ticked above, time discarded by moving hands.

I look at my Dad; sleeping more now, under an attic where lay a bundle of letters that give off a whisper of old longing and forever hope, carried across the ocean to lie above the woman who wrote them. Dad grieves and give thanks, for love still exists, even as the bones of it have crumbled to dust, becoming one with the soil, the love remains intact, impervious, where they had lain, there in the rich earth of a man's heart.

I look at a photo of my Mom, taken in the woods she loved, long before she began that fight for her life. I remember watching as a youngster, when Dad would come home to that same house, with shadowed corners and open windows, in the town where I grew up, and he'd collapse on the sofa from worry and exhaustion. Losing my mother seemed impossible; she was never as alive as in those last years when she fought so hard to stay that way. Still, death came too soon for her age, and for mine.

She is still with me daily. Whenever you've been touched by love, be it of a parent, child or friend, even after they've been taken from you, an impression is left on your heart, so that you're always reminded of the feeling of being cared for, knowing that, to someone, you mattered. You do not need a photo to remember that.

I remembered that when my Stepmom was diagnosed with Alzheimer's, a good and kind woman, lost in the shadows of her own mind, dancing to memories we could not see and crying out for those she no longer recognized. I remembered it when Big Bro was diagnosed with cancer, still fighting even though he knows who will eventually win. I remember it every day I wake up and know that even as my world dwindles, to someone, I am the form of love.

I so miss Barkley here this night, and I ask my friends to join me in saying a little prayer for him, as they have for my family this last year. There are no guarantees, but we have today. Every hour, every day is grace, even as I drive four hours to make a ramp down the back steps for a dog that will likely go out and buy a skateboard to play on it.

I am going to savor that, however. For it's not what you've lost that counts, it's what you do with what you have left, concentrating on the good things, so while we still are, we can still hope.

45
Talking to Dog

His pain had grown worse since I brought him home, another visit planned, a specialist consulted at my vet's recommendation. The last anti-inflammatory pill gone, I went to the Animal Hospital to get a refill, even though we had an appointment in two days to take another x-ray of the bone, to see if there were changes, to discuss biopsy, the doctor not ruling out bone cancer as yet.

He took it reluctantly, until I put a bit of peanut butter on it, which he then let me lay on his tongue, as if receiving a communion wafer.

I can do nothing more for him today, but relieve his pain as best I can, while I sit and stroke his flank, talking to him in a soothing voice.

I talk to my dog a lot. People would probably think me daft, sitting and talking to my dog, but outdoors or just sitting some evening quietly watching the fire, I can talk softly about the things that will matter to me the rest of my life. And he only reacts to the heat of my words or the urgency of tone as I talk about missing people I love, and the nature of death and fate and the way I've had to look hard at my own capacities to become the person I am. He just looks, and he listens.

But I also talk to God a lot.

I've certainly had to ask for that forgiveness in my talks with Him. For we talk regularly, in open fields, hunting with my Browning, when the light has a weary quality to it, like a backwater pool of light lying low, crisp and clean, illuminating everything so clearly. The words are less than wishes and more than regrets, and even if I did not state them out loud, I could hear them with my breathing as they gathered within the intent of breath and came forth in a rush of cold air, invisible words going up to an invisible God.

Sometimes He and I talk as I'm sitting in a vehicle in the middle of a scene of dark desolation, ash in my hair, red earth smeared on my boots, as bold as if painted on a door frame, a sign, that, for tonight, I was to be spared. Perhaps this one time I did not save His sparrow that He perhaps neglected to mark, but I am here to reconcile the remains. It's just talk, but it's still a prayer; prayer being more than the order of words, the conscious calling of the mind that is speaking, or the sound of the voice praying. I do not expect to hear anything back, the communication between us tongued with fire beyond the blaze that is dying next to me. But it's comforting; words spoken into the void, penitence and belief, as all around hope is falling into embers. He may not respond, but He is here, never and always, just like the four-legged form of love that lies beside me, drawing goodness even from the core of his suffering.

46

Guardians

Barkley is ever watchful, be it in the yard with a treat filled dog toy or inside.

He diligently watches the front and back doors, especially if I'm in the shower or sleeping during the day after a long trek home. He does it when we're at a friend's house.

The first time the UPS guy showed up at this address the bark was deep and ferocious, to the point the UPS guy *stopped* in his tracks on the walkway, hesitating. I cracked open the window and said "black lab!"

He smiled and came on up. I slid open the door and said, "Do you want to meet him?" He said, "Sure!" at which point Barkley came out in full "I can't handle my licker" mode and got lots of attention. I figured after that they'd be fast friends; but the next time the big brown truck showed up with a box, Barkley sounded off as if he wished to personally eat the bearer of all things Amazon.

So he sits, and he watches like some great dark stone angel.

I think of the stone angels standing above the broken flowers that are laid upon the ground at the cemetery. On any particular day, there will be a dark river of vehicles, washed and polished fluid flowing onto the grounds, circling and stopping around that depression in the earth that neither time nor sufficient airspeed will prevent our passage into. The vehicles move, almost as one, giving a sense of speed when speed itself is absent, even as those that held fast the wheels, unite in that implacable knowledge that the speed is no longer necessary.

We don't always plan on assuming the role of a guardian. Defenders and protectors are often appointed (or what we refer to as Voluntold). Some are chosen by talent and bravery, some simply because they are the only ones available.

As a small child, I was asked by my best friend to take care of her "pet" frog while she was away for the weekend with her parents. I didn't want to do it, but felt like I had to. It wasn't a real frog, being made of some stretchy, green iridescent rubber, but she loved playing with it, dubbing it an "enchanted frog" able to lift any evil spell her brother could place on her princess dolls.

Unfortunately, Mr. Frog Prince was involved in an industrial accident involving an Erector Set and the laws of physics pertaining to stretchy rubber. He lost a couple of legs as an outcome.

I was heartsick for what I'd done, especially as it was never the intent, just another childhood experiment with tools and toys. I placed the remains gently in a piece of Kleenex and put them in a box and cried my eyes out. My Mom was less than pleased and visions of Lutheran hell (which likely involved Lutefisk and 1970s gym class wear) danced in my head as she made me write my apology. I delivered it with the ruined toy and a new, better toy to replace it, paid for with my allowance for the next month.

My friend forgave me, but I did not forgive me. Not for a while.

Years later, frogs fared no better in my care, but eventually I was entrusted with not just power tools, but hearts and lives. It is why I do what I do. On my head is a ball cap with the letters of my duty. In my pocket is a piece of brass on which rests a number that will retire with me. It is shown only with respect to access those places where the sanctity and story of what remains are inviolate. In my truck is a blue lunch box that looks like the Tardis. All are parts of me, the one who will be forever the child amazed by the unknown, and the other, the one who was entrusted with something precious, determined this time, not to break it.

In another place, far away, comes a river of vehicles, mostly trucks, still flowing in toward desecrated ground. It is a landscape of scarred ground, in which the rumble of thunder and the banshee scream of the wind still echoes. Those traveling within are unprepared for what they see, a hundred streets now a single vista, with missing corners and trees whose roots now seek their moisture directly from heaven, all broken by intervals of splintered lives and stolen plans.

Through the area, there is movement, those still looking for survivors or simply what was home, here in that interchangeable section of streets without form, without remembered names. The vehicles silently pass by, in as much shock as respect. Though the vehicles bear souls inside, they also bear much more behind - water, food, diapers, wet naps, pet food, small things, even the smallest of which will fall as coins from the sky for those that have nothing.

There are times that even the bravest cannot protect, when the stoutest of hearts and the firmest of faiths cannot defend from the wrath of Mother Nature or the evil intents of humanity. But this is a land where they still trust in God even as He watches as the sky smites the earth. It is a place where they still trust in mankind's goodness, even as they know, how humans can smite innocence as well as any natural disaster. This is a place where they know that people will band together with hands and hearts and sweat and prayer, to help. Some might term those that arrive to help as angels. But they are not. They are simply flawed human beings who remember what it is like to hurt, from the pain they've received, for pain they've unwittingly caused.

The vehicles continue on to their destination, drivers pressing the foot to the gas even as they are mindful of the dangers. For on this day, speed is of the essence as there are so many waiting and needing. The vehicles try to stay together in some sense of orderly uproar, even as dust causes the eyes to weep, the remnants of bitten branches waving in a brightening sky as they pass.

They are not here specifically to protect or defend, or even, perhaps, to keep. Perhaps like Barkley, they are here, humbly and quietly, to leave some healing water for broken flowers, before heading back to home.

47

Decisions

The Internet continued with news of another weather disaster somewhere, the world no stranger to such devastation, man and Mother Nature both regularly leaving their devastating mark upon the land.

Throughout history, such dramatic events have happened; some in everyone's mind's eyes, some exposing themselves as earthquake fault lines, miles under our watchful eye, until such times as that cumulative movement suddenly erupts into our daily world. Landscapes ruptured, through history, whole cities and groups of people, lost to sight, like a coin up a magician's sleeve.

Ghost towns dot the globe; some abandoned, some retained as museums such as Oradour-sur-Glane, France. The village was destroyed in 1944; over 600 of its inhabitants were massacred by the Waffen-SS on June 10, 1944. It was said that one woman survived.

One.

Things that change the course of a landscape and its people usually start small. Deep in the Sahara Desert, a column of hot air swirls upward fifteen thousand feet, spreading as it races to the west coast where it dips toward the ocean. This small-bit player, coached by the flow of the ocean, the spin of the air and the accolades of warm water, soon grows into a hurricane that slams into the Gulf Coast, setting up the act and the scene before the curtain even had time to fall.

But what of the dinosaurs, the largest creatures to ever walk this earth? It is said they were felled by an unseen comet, something oceans wide that disrupted the earth. Or perhaps it was just one small burp in the ecosphere, like the invisible microbe that ended the Martians in the War of the Worlds. Was it only one thing, or one giant calamitous thing that emptied the monuments and granaries and empiric towers of the Mayans? For they left, with no clues left behind, no words, and no records, entire cities whose names and artifacts hinted of exotic riches and excesses, nothing remaining but a soundless roar of a civilization vanished.

What was it? Did something tremendous happen that required immediate action, and were they struck down, hypnotized under the glare of that great and enduring *was*. Or did they look from the corner of their eyes, a flash of movement, a small thing actually, the small, shiny blade of change, and flee from it, never to return.

Sometimes it *is* the small things. It is a branch of coral comprised of uncountable polyps that together, form a living thing.

It is living yeast that combines with flour and liquid and the labor of hands to make bread. It is the opposing and orthogonal perspective of myriad pieces of metal, formed into a useful function by the human mind. It's one small bird taking flight, joining another, and another, until the sky is dark with their winged victory.

It's a small black puppy in a well-worn photograph. It's another photo, of a red haired woman with that same dog, now old and grey. Between those two pictures, there was much love, so much life.

Sometimes it's the big things, the sun that peeks up over the horizon each morning, millions of people turning to that same spot in which they gaze upon their expectation. A figure nailed upon a cross, all those many eyes, looking in that one direction, saying the same litany of prayer, with the same prostrations. Father, Son and Holy Ghost, Amen; cleansing us in the fire, as worlds away a wall of rain and wind condense and compound to wash away more than sin.

The heavens contain pieces of satellite that may fall to earth, each of them capable of harm, each capable of simply dropping into the ocean where their presence will not be noticed or missed. What will happen to them as they enter the atmosphere, as they cross the line that separates the unknown from the comprehended? Will we even notice?

I would not notice. For all that fills my view is a diagnosis, the one we did not want to hear, even as it was spoken, with a voice tinged in tears.

In a small bed, lies a beloved dog, weary of battles both large and small, yet refusing to give quarter against a foe just the size of one cell of his body. Each and every cell in return put up its own fight, even as some were sacrificed to the cause, the body on fire from within itself. I watched the struggle to rise from his bed with the pain. I watched him try and hide it, lapping up every bit of joy despite the wellspring of his suffering. I watched him play in the face of that fire and continue the fight that he will lose, still with that invisible captaincy of spirit that is as infinite in capacity as it is in faith.

Everything worth meaning is made up of so many small parts, its moments, its words, its acts, the skin and bone and the nucleus within us that contains its own fire, somewhere deep inside. We're our own walking fate, and we're our own little miracles, the atoms from which we're made; not so different from the atoms of the earth, the air, the water, all of us formed from that blazing nucleus of the stars—Heaven, binding us together.

I will never fully understand the miracle that is our existence, our role in the vast wonder that is earth and space and Heaven. But I can grasp the wonder of my world, in a volcanic rock formed in the earth that holds in place letters from a loved one long ago, in a pressed leaf in a photo frame; the tiny veins within it stilled, a leaf once green, held tight between pages. It died in the loss of a battle between promise and poison, leaving just the shell of what was once a beautiful thing.

I look at my own hands, the web of veins, the flow and beat of my blood, frailer than the scent of copper and louder than the seethe and fury of the ocean. I think of the decision I must make, not tomorrow, but today.

48

Goodbye

The drive from the vet to home was as long as a lifetime, a collar and leash, lying on the back seat where only hours ago, lay someone so excited to be going to the vet, never afraid of that place, only happy for the extra attention and special treats.

Can I live with the drive, knowing he would never return?

There is no pain, no regrets. Everything I gave him, he gave me back ten fold, listening to me chat away about my day, things that by my oath of duty, I couldn't tell anyone else. He was my black knight with wagging tail. He was the finder of slippers and the keeper of hearts.

He was a dog, but he was much more than a dog.

He was support, he was patience. He was the promise that, even with the worst mistakes, he still loved me. He was that fire that cauterized me against loneliness and fear, the thump of his tail like the sound of a heart in the womb, creature comfort there in the dark and unknown. He became the unevictable place in a heart so bruised it had pushed everyone harshly away that got too close. He taught me to trust again. With that trust, I found my heart's twin, who happily became his family as well.

As a family, we take care of each other. Having a pet is a commitment just as is any bond, either visible or invisible with another living creature. It's not just being a good friend during the good times, it's being a friend during surgery, explosive doggrhea, and that pile of vomit in the corner on the one square of carpet that wasn't protected by a cheap throw rug.

You do what you can to help them during those scary, shadowed times, with tender, soothing words. You don't lay your hand upon them with forceful curse and belittlement. They look at you to be the strong one, the better one, even if it's difficult to do. They trust you to act from your heart and not from the infinite, internal voices of human fear and angst.

They pay it back in ways that can't be captured, but by the measured beat of a tail. On those nights when you come home really, really late from work, your soul weary, the house dark, they will quietly come up to you, leaning into you, drawn from their slumber to your side like steel and magnet. At that moment, there as both your hearts beat in the silence, you realize that every measure of sickness and health was worth it.

For there is a great measure of trust and love contained in that warm web of bone and fur, the eyes that can commandeer your pancakes and the tail that wags for you as if you were the only person on the planet for them, and maybe you are.

Their time is so short, indeed, but that does not mean you should not love. In "people" years, Barkley was probably sixty something. But they were years condensed down into their core elements, as if a simple ordinary succession of days were not enough, as if the love and all of that faithfulness, the freedom of the field, and the tug of a leash toward the horizon was compressed down into something as hard and brilliant as a diamond. Everything, every single element of so many long days is there in that short span of time, compounded into that one leap, one surge, toward the lights of a vehicle in the drive, one joyous bark that contains within it simply, "My person is home."

He cared nothing about where we lived, how I looked, or how much money was in the bank. All he cared about was how to bequeath that which sustained him, in his too short life, his faith and his love, as he patiently waited for my return.

When he greeted me, he seemed to know when I just needed to sit in the quiet. He seemed to know when I wanted to play. If there were a ball to be thrown, he would abandon all restraint and gave every fiber of himself, to reach for that which was before only a dream--unmitigated glory. His life was not deadlines, or deals, or caring about the things that in, all reality, will not matter at the end of life. His life was simply a joyous run ahead of that avalanche of time that would be his enemy had he any concept of it.

But time caught up with him, forcing a decision that I hoped wouldn't have to be made. The bone cancer diagnosis was in and final. Medication could not keep the pain at bay and amputation and chemo were only going to buy a very short amount of time, at the expense of his comfort. I could not in good conscience make him go through that, for there was no cure, only a continuation of pain. So I was there, by his side, not passing on the burden to someone in a white lab coat, loving and caring, but not his "Mom." Although we never formally took an oath, paw placed upon a revered document, flag on the wall, an oath was taken. When he came home with me as a puppy, he swore his life to serve and protect. That was his duty, as it is mine.

He had enough medication to briefly take the pain away, a big bowl of food that wasn't kibble, and all the treats he could happily gobble down. There was no fear in him, no pain, and no anxiety. Dad and Mom said goodbye as I placed my cool hand on his warm flank and talked to him down at floor level, looking into his eyes, in all those murmured words that meant something only to us. Where else could I be but to just be there as the needle quietly slipped in and he was set free from all burden, one surge, one leap toward the light so easily and joyously, so as to lose all sense of restraint, weightless upon the warm, invisible air. He was free, the pain of bone and flesh departed, only one long, joyous, soundless bark as he went Home to wait by the Rainbow Bridge until we can catch up.

He was more than a dog. He was love that crept in on four paws and remains, as long as memory lasts.

49

Ghosts

After the death of Barkley, I received this note from a female friend, a sailor and adventurer with an indomitable spirit:

"When I was 18, I lost my lifelong companion Sally – with me since birth, a small black and white cocker mix, my best and sometimes only friend. She loved me, I believe, more perfectly than I could ever have loved her in my inexperience. When she was 18 she died and I grieved and I cried and I still get tears in my eyes when I think of that sweet little soul who gave me so much. So no, you never get over it. I do not know anyone who has loved a dog and has said goodbye that gets over it. The pain? As you know, it eases, it becomes sweet memory with time, and you still get tears in your eyes, but the smiles and laughter at the remembered fun and antics of your 4-legged Pal returns to you.

"My mother is part Iroquois, and although a lifelong Catholic, carried with her some of the mythology handed down in her family. She knew my grief was raw and painful and that only time would help heal the wound in my heart. 'She said to me 'Sally walks with you and with time, she will allow you to feel her there

beside you. During the first time of grief, you are blind to her and that is as it should be, so she will know she is no longer in This World, but now walks in the Spirit World. When you are ready, she will help ease your pain by showing you memories, and helping you laugh again when you are ready to see that she is not lost to you, but always remains a part of you. Your tears will then be tears of joy at your good fortune at having known such a one.'"

Those words brought me much comfort, even as I did not dream of him. Sleep through the night was finally occurring, even as I woke expecting to feel the touch of cold snoot against my hand: "Get up Mom; get up, Mom; it's time for Dog Food again!"

But those first few weeks, there were no dreams. Last night, alone while my husband was on the road, one finally came. In my dream, I got up from sleep, wandered out into the hall and there he was, standing there in the bright morning light. I *knew* I was dreaming, and I also knew he was gone from this world, I stared at what, to me in my slumbering musings was a ghost Barkley.

I felt tears well up, then I noticed that look on his face, a look of guilt and somewhat pride, an, "Oh No, look what I just did!" and "Wow, that's the biggest one yet," all in one expression.

There in the shadowed corners of the room, where the rug was indelibly stained from such earlier occurrences was a big fresh pile of dog vomit. Ghost Barkley had come back to leave me a little gift.

I woke up, to an empty room and clean floors, laughing as, from outside, the sound of the winged birds of morning began.

I hope he will come to me in future dreams, but if not, I will not remember the dog barf, dreamed or otherwise, the accidents, the dog hair, chewed clothing, and the remnants of the only expensive pair of shoes I ever bought.

I will remember him, standing there in the light with the reconciled luminousness of angels in stained glass, their form, a four-legged one lacking wings but not their saving Grace. The light upon him was so bright, that when I looked at it, the body of the dog and face had clarity, almost brilliance, but without form or dimension, no longer animal, no longer flesh and heart and bone, but simply the brilliant inherent capacity to love as fully and as freely as possible.

That is the way I wish to remember him. His Light.

As I come home tonight, I understand that he is not here. Still, as I step up the steps, I desperately want to hear the soft "*woof*" of a black lab, waiting in the kitchen for me to step in. But I can only approach, in that utter quiet that is now the house, sensing those who are absent, who inhabited this place but exist now as only ghosts of my past living on the breath of memory.

I stand outside the door, hearing hushed wind, hand on the doorknob, hesitant to open the door to every memory, more hesitant to leave them behind. I stand there silently, my presence not detected by dogs forever silent, motionless, trying to blend in with the house, the dark wood and trees, listening to the living presence of a home, all the lives and love and heartache that went into it, that formed these four walls, that now form me.

I listen, as a churchgoer does, to chants in ancient languages that no one understands, but listens to anyway, the words a peace that flows like water. There is no bark but that of the trees, and the baleful sound of a wind that speaks the name of one departed. I listen for things I'd dream of, if only I could sleep.

I open up the door to go on in. I have no words for what I am feeling. I have no name for the quiet that waits inside. But that is OK. There are no names for the sun's warmth on the skin; of the trinity of earth and sky and water. There are no names for the bones that lie in quiet mourning, bringing riches to the earth. There are no names for the rocks that direct a stream's flow, for the fur and leaves that line an eagle's nest. Yet they are, and always will be. Strong. Necessary. Waiting.

50

Learning to Walk on Broken Glass

"One day some people came to the master and asked 'How can you be happy in a world of such impermanence, where you cannot protect your loved ones from harm, illness and death?' The master held up a glass and said 'Someone gave me this glass, and I really like this glass. It holds my water admirably and it glistens in the sunlight. I touch it and it rings! One day the wind may blow it off the shelf, or my elbow may knock it from the table. I know this glass is already broken, so I enjoy it incredibly." – Achaan Chah Subato – Theravandan meditation master

As children, we view the world as if it will always be as it is that day. Mom and Dad will always be there; the dog will live forever. There is little that cannot be fixed by glue, a bandage and Mom's chocolate chip cookies. As we get older, those perceptions sometimes still remain, that we will live happily ever after; we will have children, who will have children, who will have children, the family living forever, in defined order of aging and passing. We go into adulthood believing what is useful for us to believe, or rather what is intolerable for us *not* to believe.

After the death of Barkley, we went out to see my Dad, to laugh and remember, much more than the life of a dog. One day while I was there, I took Dad and my new husband up to the cemetery on top of a hill, where we could watch our shadows upon two small graves. Big Bro did not go, still weary from both chemo and radiation, but helped us prepare flowers to take to those graves.

I remember standing there, shafts of sun hitting that small stone, listening to the short song of a bird hidden, who sang four short notes then ceased, as from a distance came the incurious, calm sound of bells. As my Dad did, I realized long ago, that one must sometimes don that mantle of flame, which we do not have the power to remove but only to bear, without being devoured by the blaze.

There is no perfect order, there is no guarantee, but there still is, and always will be, beauty. If we didn't learn that, we'd only move without living and grieve without weeping, neither worth the toll they take on that which remains. For myself, I chose now to weep, and, with that, remember.

I think again to those beliefs peculiar to childhood, namely those things we believe, simply because we are yet too young not to believe. The first was Santa Claus. I had my doubts that first year I sat on Santa's lap at the hardware store and he had on black geek glasses. Santa should look like Santa, not a 30-year-old CPA. Still I kept it quiet, buying Mom's explanation that he was just Santa's stunt double, Santa being busy that day. Certainly Santa was real, he had to be real.

Then there was the Tooth Fairy. Dad still has this little note, written in my handwriting, an affidavit to the Tooth Fairy attesting that indeed I did lose my tooth, but I swallowed it with the piece of apple that pried it loose. It's wrapped around a little plastic box filled with baby teeth. Big Bro was a little less subtle. One night, long after I was asleep, Dad was alerted from the bathroom where he was preparing for bed with a "Dad, I caught the Tooth Fairy," and he had Mom by the arm and was tickling her and they were *both* laughing.

The Easter bunny had just a slight role at Easter, being a tradition to bring sweets to celebrate the gift and the Sacrifice of Jesus, rather than being the reason for the whole holiday. Still, before church, we loved to find the little baskets outside the door, with candy eggs and a chocolate bunny. Until one day, when we got up, and there was no basket.

Mom and Dad announced we were too old for the Easter Bunny. Instead, they were taking us on an outing tomorrow! To the State Capital! Yes, children getting to visit a government building instead of receiving a basket of candy! You can only imagine our excitement. On the drive there, we whispered intricate conspiracies from the back seat to get out of this, to no avail, not wanting to hurt our Mom's feelings. So we learned what a rotunda was and Dad finagled a tour at a local brewery on the way back, likely needing a drink after watching our tax dollars in action.

Watching the cans getting processed was a whole lot more fun than politicians in suits, and as we drove home, Mom did stop and get us some ice cream, realizing the day hadn't gone as she'd hoped but appreciating that we at least tried. I think deep down we had known for some time the Easter Bunny was our Mom and Dad. But we were not yet openly willing to admit to another fractured fairy tale.

Still though, our parents let us hold on to the perception that the world was unbroken as long as they could. Some things, though, could not wait until adulthood. One was finding out we were adopted. So many people, then, and even now, ask me about biological parents, and I have no answers for them. But for the reason of the severing of that tie, which is not the concern of the world, neither of us sought to find them, outside the scope of our hurt or their harm, even if we refused to pass judgment for the reasons we ended up where we did. Or perhaps we did pass judgment, but were simply unwilling to pronounce sentence.

All I can truly say is my brother and I came into the best possible family. Disciplined, loving, hard working people that came from nothing by way of material means or privilege and still crafted a life of learning and beauty. Our clothes were handed down, or handmade, our food from the garden, or the fields nearby, our bikes used. But we had everything that was truly important, and that was a deep appreciation for every day, even those marked with illness or rain, easily forgotten when we were greeted upon returning home by Mom's smile and the joyous bark of a dog.

This was the beauty of family, simultaneously fragmented and undefeated, emboldened and afraid, yet still seeing the good in the world around us. So we carry on, my brother and I, as we tell our stories. "Remember when Dad was told to give me the 'birds and the bees, boys and girls are different talk' because Mom was sick? It consisted of a photo of a boy from the Sears catalog in his underwear, a finger pointed to a critical area and the admonishment 'Don't kick your brother there!'" He would then laugh and remind me of something silly I had done in school, memories that shone in the sunlight on the telling, his laughter still ringing like a touch on glass. In our stories, we are children and our favorite dog is always with us. We are not just immortal; we are invincible. We will run and run until our bones turn to water, and we fall in a puddle of arms and legs and barking dog, forever joyful.

On the wall of the family room is a family tree that my aunt drew out with careful calligraphy, giving us each a copy. I note many branches, some ending abruptly as some died young, some were widowed, some childless, a lifelong bachelor or spinster among them. Now on a branch, which had ended abruptly, is a name, next to mine, something I owe in part to a dog named Barkley.

For Barkley was indeed my family, his story joining these others, each entwined into a family history of black sheep, white knights, the victors, the vanquished, each carrying with them loves and burdens and more than one four-legged companion with which they shared the journey. Each name, name by name and page by page, will be laid down until inevitably, only one name will remain, for that glass is indeed, inevitably broken. That person will, I hope, capture the names, and whisper the stories that haunt the winds, even if no one is left to hear, but ghosts on the page, with no earthly house in which they wait for us.

As I start to weep my brother touches my face, in benediction, in blessing. That is the true beauty which sustains us; that His sacrifice through which the world was saved is re-enacted here in this world every day, in the saving grace of a small imperfect family and the memory of a dog.